Sexually Violent Predator
An Inside Look Into the KSVPA Statute and Facility

By
Dustin Merryfield

CP

Cadmus Publishing
www.cadmuspublishing.com

Published by Cadmus Publishing
www.cadmuspublishing.com
Port Angeles, WA

ISBN: 978-1-63751-203-6

CONTENTS

Introduction to the Book

It is my hope that this book will shed light on a subject that appeals to almost every person in the world. I know there are those that hate a sex offender and there are those that believe the past is the past and one can change and then there are those that have been labeled a Sexually Violent Predator, the most feared and hated person in the United States.

For those who hate sex offenders this book will cause them to agree with the inflictions shown and believe more needs to be inflicted. However, as a human is this the right way to think? I do not believe so and instead it should be the sex offender hater who wants reform to the point that such a program stays in existence.

For those who are the family of a loved one in the same situation or who feel that no matter what the past a person should not be treated unfairly or improperly this book will give them cause to want reform.

No matter which type you are, keep in mind you are a tax payer and it is your money that funds such programs in the United States. This book will show where if you demand certain reform the cost to your pocketbook would be lessened for the cost of the program would be less.

With all of this in mind I do not discredit anyone for their thoughts or beliefs and only want to be the one that enlightens all. In addition the bonus would be that reform in these types of places occurs across the United States.

Thank you very much for taking the time to read this and enjoy.

PART I: THE AUTHOR

CHAPTER 1

BECOMING A PREDATOR

—⟶○◖⟋◗○⟵—

In order to be committed under the Kansas Sexually Violent Predator Act (KSVPA), statute K.S.A. § 59-29a01 et seq., one must have been charged with or convicted of a specific sex crime and have a mental abnormality or personality disorder that causes them to lack control over sexual offending.

I was placed in the State of Kansas system at the age of ten as a child in need of care. This caused me to be placed in different facilities. Based on my behavior in the facility determined whether or not I was moved. In my case I was a problem this caused me to be moved from location to location. I had spent time in places such as: Topeka State Hospital, Charter of Wichita, Cowley County Youth Shelter, and Pawnee Valley in Newton Kansas.

While on partial release I offended against an employee of the facility. She was eighteen and I was thirteen. For this sexual assault I was charged with Rape. I was sentenced to the Youth Center at Larned (YCAL). While in YCAL I assaulted and battered staff and other confined persons and destroyed property. For this I was sent to the Youth Center at Topeka (YCAT). At YCAT I straightened up and began receiving treatment until they let me go.

The youth prisons in Kansas were being transferred from the Department of Social and Rehabilitation Services to the Juvenile Justice Authority. As part of the change certain individuals were released with only a two day notice. I was one released.

I was living at home and partaking of normal life events. However, I did not have to go to school for I had already graduated High School. I had a job and was starting my life. Then I was at a park and touched a child in an inappropriate manner. For this I was sentenced to the Kansas Department of Corrections (KDOC) as an adult at the age of seventeen (17).

Near the end of my time in KDOC, at the age of eighteen (18), the multidisciplinary team met with me to determine if they should recommend me for commitment under the KSVPA. I was evaluated by B.L. Atkinson who held the following: "Making Recommendations for Mr. Merryfield is difficult, because he has so little base to build on. He needs structure and guidance in many areas, but will be overwhelmed by programs and counselors."

The McPherson County Sheriff picked me up at the KDOC facility a few days before my release to be tried as a Sexually Violent Predator (SVP).

During the proceeding I was evaluated by the Larned State Hospital's evaluator Rex Rosenberg. Later in his career he was found to be mentally ill and found to have been seeing demons. This calls into question the validity of his evaluation that recommended I fit the criteria to be committed under the KSVPA.

The next evaluation was done by an outside professional, Dr. Richard Irons, he held the following: "In my professional opinion he has not attained a level of developmental maturity or basic impulse control to get sufficient benefit from a sex offenders treatment program. I would recommend as an alternative that resources be used to obtain treatment and rehabilitation for his conduct disorder and within that program provide treatment for his sexual misconduct that would be given to an adolescent offender."

After the evaluations the Court held a bench trial and committed me.

I became an SVP for the past two offenses at the age of eighteen and thirteen then entered into the program in the year 2000. This is how I became a predator.

Chapter 2

My Background

I grew up in a small town with a broken home. My biological dad was a drunk and convicted felon that was in and out of the picture. In came a myriad of step fathers. I lived at home and eventually went to the family farm. At the age of ten I became a ward of the state.

Once I was a ward of the state I bounced around from place to place. I was always being moved because I was causing problems or hurting others. Some of the places I had been were Bob Johnson's, Charter Hospital, Topeka State Hospital, Youth Center at Larned, Youth Center at Topeka and Prairie View.

I always struggled in school and got in trouble more at school than anywhere. It was not until I attended high school in the Youth Center at Topeka, that a teacher recognized that I had an ability to quickly learn material. This was causing the issues for me in school for I was bored and the learning was too slow. I was moved to a self-paced study which allowed me to rapidly earn my credits. Eventually I left high school and received my G.E.D.

After receiving my G.E.D. I went to many vocational and trade school programs and received certificates in Computers, Life Rescue, Horticulture, and Family Planning, to name a few. After a few years of this I went back to school and got my High School Diploma in the Youth Center at Topeka.

At the age of seventeen I went to prison as an adult for my second offense. I did about a year in prison and then was tried under the KSVPA. About a year later at the age of eighteen I walked in the front door of the Sexual Predator Treatment Program in Kansas.

At the Sexual Predator Treatment Program I have earned my college degrees. In or about the year 2003 I started taking courses for my Associate's in Applied Computer Science. I completed three of the four semesters. About the same time I earned a Diploma in PC Repair.

I started college again in late 2019 and since then I have earned a Paralegal Degree, Associate's and bachelor's in Theology, and working on the completion of a second Paralegal Degree and an advanced Paralegal Degree in business. I am also back in school earning my degree in business. I have graduated with honors and maintain an average of a 4.0 GPA.

I spend my time in the facility researching law, doing civil litigation, working in the facility, and playing video games. I do attend one-hundred percent of my treatment and have even advanced to the pre-release stage and was returned for a rule violation. I did violate the rule and now must work for pre-release again.

PART II: THE STATUTORY ACT

CHAPTER 1

HISTORICAL BACKGROUND OF THE KSVPA

———————— ⇌◦ᏨᏨᏰᏰ◦⇌ ————————

K ansas's 1994 Sexually Violent Predator Act (S.B.525), was passed in response to the high profile rape and murder of a young college student named Stephanie Schmidt by a convicted sex offender.

The legislative record contained no information or data that was ever presented about the post-release danger of sex offenders as a class. There was one three-page fragment of an article on self-reported career histories of sex offenders which was reproduced twice in the records, but it did not cover the post-release records of offenders. This omission matters because SVP legislation is premised on the idea that persons will continue to reoffend even after they have been formally held accountable by the state for a sexually predatory crime. In addition, although two witnesses made factual assertions about multiple victim career offenders, they did not provide support for their testimony.

On February 22, 1994, Kansas Attorney General Carla Stovall testified that "an FBI study of serial rapists showed an average of 20 rapes each in their history," but she provided no reference to the source and no indication of how this information would impact the population covered by S.B. 525.

Representative Gary Haulmark--a member of the Ad Hoc Sexual Offender Task Force created in the wake of Schmidt's murder that recommended S.B. 525 to the legislature--testified that "our task force saw statistic after statistic which indicated that these people will reoffend 50% to 90% of the time if allowed the opportunity." Like Stovall, Haulmark did not reference any specific study. Nor was there any data presented by the Kansas Department of Corrections on sex offender recidivism.

Although a former member of the state's Parole Commission testified in favor of the bill, he did not provide any data to support his position. Indeed, no prison release follow-ups of any class of sex offender were requested by the legislative committees considering S.B. 525, much less actually submitted to the House or Senate committees. The release and parole data could have shown the danger posed by Kansas's sex offenders.

CHAPTER 2

LEGISLATIVE HISTORY OF THE ACT

⸺⸺⸺⸺⸺⸻⟡⟡⟡⟡⸻⸺⸺⸺⸺⸺

The KSVPA was enacted by Senate Bill 525 in 1994. At the time of its creation it contained a total of sixteen (16) sections.

On June 23, 1997 the United States Supreme Court issued its decision in Kansas v. Hendricks, 521 U.S. 346. This decision rendered a determination that the KSVPA was constitutionally permissible, in a narrow decision for the Court was split 5-4.

Today there are twenty-nine sections in the KSVPA. This means there is about eighty-one (81) percent of the KSVPA that is new since the review by the U.S. Supreme Court in Kansas v. Hendricks.

Up until the time the U.S. Supreme Court rendered its decision the Legislature only amended the KSVPA nine (9) times. After the decision the Legislature amended the KSVPA a total of sixty-seven (67) times. A total of seventy-six (76) amendments have occurred.

Chapter 3

Legislative Amendments to the KSVPA

———————— ⊸o⟨⟋⟍⟍⊸o⟨ ————————

I. K.S.A. § 59-29a01

K.S.A. § 59-29a01 was enacted in 1994 and prior to the decision in Hendricks was never amended, post Hendricks the statute was amended twice.

In the year 1999 the Kansas Legislature passed House Bill 2101. Specifically: changed it to state: "The legislature finds that there exists an extremely dangerous group of sexually violent predators who have a mental abnormality or personality disorder and who are likely to engage in repeat acts of sexual violence if not treated for their mental abnormality or personality disorder. Because the existing civil commitment procedures under K.S.A. 59-2901 et seq. and amendments thereto are inadequate to address the special needs of sexually violent predators and the risks they present to society, the legislature determines that a separate involuntary civil commitment process for the potentially long-term control, care and treatment of sexually violent predators is necessary. The legislature also determines that because of the nature of the mental abnormalities or personality disorders from which sexually violent predators suffer, and the dangers they present, it is necessary to house involuntarily committed sexually violent predators in an environment separate from persons involuntarily committed under K.S.A. 59-2901 et. seq., and amendments thereto."

In the year 2003 the Kansas Legislature passed Senate Bill 27. Specifically it added the following language: "Notwithstanding any other evidence of legislative intent, it is hereby declared that any time requirements set forth in K.S.A. 59-29a01 et seq., and amendments thereto, either as originally enacted or as amended, are intended to be directory and not mandatory and serve as guidelines for conducting proceedings under K.S.A. 59-29a01 et seq., and amendments thereto."

II. K.S.A. § 59-29a02

K.S.A. § 59-29a02 was enacted in 1994 and prior to the decision in Hendricks was amended only once, post Hendricks the statute was amended seven times. This part of the KSVPA is known as the Definitions Statute.

In the year 1995 the Kansas Legislature passed Senate Bill 3. Specifically it Added the words "if not confined in a secure facility," at the end of the definition of a Sexually Violent Predator. It also Added the Kansas Parole Board to the definition of "Agency with Jurisdiction."

In the year 1998 the Kansas Legislature passed Senate Bill 671. Specifically it added four new definitions as follows:

"Person" means an individual who is a potential or actual subject of proceedings under this act.

"Treatment staff" means the persons, agencies or firms employed by or contracted with the secretary to provide treatment, supervision or other services at the sexually violent predator facility.

"Transitional release" means any halfway house, work release or other placement designed to assist the person's adjustment and reintegration into the community once released from commitment.

"Secretary" means the secretary of the department of social and rehabilitation services

In the year 1999 the Kansas Legislature passed House Bill 2101. Specifically in the definition of Sexually Violent Predator removed the word "predatory" and replaced it with the word "repeat." It also removed the definition of "predatory" and replaced it with "likely to engage in repeat acts of sexual violence" means the person's propensity to commit acts of sexual violence is of such a degree as to pose a menace to the health and safety of others.

In the year 2006 the Kansas Legislature passed Senate Bill 506. Specifically it added the words "Sexually Violent Predator Treatment Facility" to the definition of transition.

In the year 2011 the Kansas Legislature passed House Bill 2339. This showed that the criminal code in the Statute books for Kansas moved to another section.

In the year 2012 the Kansas Legislature passed House Bill 2535. Specifically changing from the use of Kansas Parole Board to prisoner review board.

In the year 2014 the Kansas Legislature passed House Bill 2515. This the change where the state went from the use of Department of Social and Rehabilitation Services to Kansas Department for Aging and Disability Services or Secretary for Aging and Disability Services.

In the year 2018 the Kansas Legislature passed Senate Bill 266. Specifically it added to the definition of sexually violent predator the words: "and who has serious difficulty in controlling such person's dangerous behavior" then it added three new definitions as follows:

"Conditional release" means approved placement in the community for a minimum of five years while under the supervision of the person's court of original commitment and monitored by the secretary for aging and disability services.

"Conditional release monitor" means an individual appointed by the court to monitor the person's compliance with the treatment plan while placed on conditional release and who reports to the court. Such monitor shall not be a court services officer.

"Progress review panel" means individuals appointed by the

secretary for aging and disability services to evaluate a person's progress in the sexually violent predator treatment program.

III. K.S.A. § 59-29a03

K.S.A. § 59-29a03 was enacted in 1994 and prior to the decision in Hendricks was amended only twice, post Hendricks the statute was amended two times. This part of the KSVPA is known as the Notice of Release statute.

In the year 1995 the Kansas Legislature passed Senate Bill 3. Concerning this it changed from the prosecuting attorney to the Attorney General as the legal representative in the proceedings for the State. Added a provision that allows for one who is returned to be prison for a parole or post release supervision violation to be tried under the KSVPA near the end of their ninety day re-confinement period. It also created and added the multidisciplinary team and prosecutor's review committed to the KSVPA proceeding and required that the Secretary of KDOC or Attorney General establish one..

In the year 1995 the Kansas Legislature passed House Bill 2223. Concerning this it added that one found guilty of a non-sexually violent offense, but the jury returns it was sexually motivated is allowed to be tried under the KSVPA.

In the year 1999 the Kansas Legislature passed House Bill 2101. Concerning this it added the following language: "(F) the provisions of this section are not jurisdictional, and failure to comply with such provisions in no way prevents the attorney general from proceeding against a person otherwise subject to the provision of K.S.A. 59-29a01 et seq., and amendments thereto."

In the year 2015 the Kansas Legislature passed Senate Bill 12. Concerning this it added the following language:

"(c) Any reports of evaluations prepared or provided pursuant to subsection (b) shall demonstrate that the person evaluated was informed of the following:(1) the nature and purpose of the evaluation; and (2) that the evaluation will not be confidential and that any statements made by the person and any conclusions drawn by the evaluator may be disclosed to a court, the detained person's attorney, the prosecutor and the Trier of fact at any proceeding conducted under the Kansas Sexually Violent Predator Act."

"(d) The permitted disclosures required to be submitted to the attorney general under this section shall be deemed to be in response to the attorney general's civil demand for relevant and material information to investigate whether a petition shall be filed. The information provided shall be specific to the purposes of the Kansas Sexually Violent Predator Act and as limited in scope as reasonably practicable."

Senate Bill 12 also required that the Multidisciplinary Team include the mental health professional who prepared any evaluation, interviewed the person or made any recommendation to the attorney general. It also corrected the previous language added to state: "The provisions of this section are not jurisdictional and failure to comply with such provisions not affecting constitutional rights in no way prevents the attorney general from proceeding against a person otherwise subject to the provision of K.S.A. 59-29a01 et seq. and amendments thereto provisions of the Kansas Sexually Violent Predator Act."

IV. K.S.A. § 59-29a04

K.S.A. § 59-29a04 was enacted in 1994 and prior to the decision in Hendricks was amended only once, post Hendricks the statute was amended four times. This part of the KSVPA is known as the Petition statute.

In the year 1995 the Kansas Legislature passed Senate Bill 3. Concerning this it removed county prosecutor and replaced it with the prosecutor's review committee established by the attorney general.

In the year 1999 the Kansas Legislature passed House Bill 2101. Concerning this it added the following language: "(b) the provisions of this section are not jurisdictional, and failure to comply with such provisions in no way prevents the attorney general from proceeding against a person otherwise subject to the provision of K.S.A. 59-29a01 et seq., and amendments thereto."

In the year 2003 the Kansas Legislature passed Senate Bill 27. Concerning this it added the following language: "May file a petition in the county where the person was convicted of or charged with a sexually violent offense."

In the year 2007 the Kansas Legislature passed Senate Bill 52. Concerning this it added the following language: "(c) Whenever a determination is made regarding whether a person may be a sexually violent predator, the county responsible for the costs incurred, including, but not limited to costs of investigation, prosecution, defense, juries, witness fees and expenses, expert fees and expenses and other expenses related to determining whether a person may be a sexually violent predator shall be reimbursed for such costs by the office of the attorney general from the sexually violent predator expense fund. The attorney general shall develop and implement a procedure to provide such reimbursements. If there are no moneys available in such fund to pay any such reimbursements, the county may file a claim against the state pursuant to Article 9 of chapter 46, of the Kansas Statutes Annotated, and amendments thereto."

In the year 2015 the Kansas Legislature passed Senate Bill 12. Concerning this it added the following language: "(b) Notwithstanding the provisions of subsection (a), when the person named in the petition is a person who has been convicted of or charged with a federal or other state offense that under the laws of this state would be a sexually violent offense, as defined in K.S.A. 59-29a02, and amendments thereto, the attorney general may file the petition in the county where the person now resides, was charged or convicted of any offense, or was released. (c) Service of the petition on the attorney appointed or hired to represent the person shall be deemed sufficient service."

V. K.S.A. § 59-29a04a

K.S.A. § 59-29a04a was enacted in 2007, ten years after the decision in Hendricks, post Hendricks the statute was amended two times. This part of the KSVPA is known as the Sexually Violent Predator Expense Fund statute.

In the year 2007, the Legislature created a new section in the KSVPA, Senate Bill 52, and listed it as K.S.A. § 59-29a04a, Sexual Predator Expense Fund (hereinafter SPEF). It created the SPEF and placed the

Attorney General in charge of the account. It was to be used to pay for costs related to determining whether and individual is an SVP.

The first amendment to this occurred in the year 2011, House Bill 2071, and it added that the expenses or costs of any Habeas Corpus filed by one committed as an SVP was to be paid out of the SPEF.

The second amendment was in 2015, Senate Bill 12, and it changed the language from Habeas Corpus to any civil action.

VI. K.S.A. § 59-29a05

K.S.A. § 59-29a05 was enacted in 1994 and prior to the decision in Hendricks was amended only once, post Hendricks the statute was amended two times. This part of the KSVPA is known as the Probable Cause statute.

In the year 1995 the Kansas Legislature passed Senate Bill 3. Concerning this it added the following language: "(b) Within 72 hours after a person is taken into custody pursuant to subsection (a), such person shall be provided with notice of, and an opportunity to appear in person at, a hearing to contest probable cause as to whether the detained person is a sexually violent predator. At this hearing the court shall: (1) verify the detainer's identity; and (2) determine whether probable cause exists to believe that the person is a sexually violent predator. The state may rely upon the petition and supplement the petition with additional documentary evidence or live testimony. (c) At the probable cause hearing as provided in subsection (b), the detained person shall have the following rights in addition to the rights previously specified: (1) to be represented by counsel; (2) to present evidence on such person's behalf; (3) to cross-examine witnesses who testify against such person; and (4) to view and copy all petitions and reports in the court file. "

Senate Bill 3 also added a clause allowing for the person to be housed in the county jail.

In the year 2012 the Kansas Legislature passed Senate Bill 280. Concerning this it added the following language: "(e) The person conducting the evaluation ordered by the court pursuant to this section shall notify the detained person of the following: (1) The nature and purpose of the evaluation; and (2) that the evaluation will not be confidential and that any statements made by the detained person, and any conclusions drawn by the evaluator, will be disclosed to the court, the detained person's attorney, the prosecutor and the Trier of fact at any proceeding conducted under K.S.A. 59-29a01 et seq., and amendments thereto."

In the year 2015 the Kansas Legislature passed Senate Bill 12. Concerning this it added language that requires one being tried under the KSVPA to be housed in a county jail until the determination is made, once a petition for commitment is filed. It also required that the judge enter a protective order, once the petition is filed, permitting disclosures of protected health information to the parties, their counsel, evaluators, experts and others necessary to the litigation during the course of the proceedings subject to the KSVPA.

Senate Bill 12 also changed the requirement that a probable cause hearing be held within seventy-two hours, to as soon as reasonably practicable or agreed upon by the parties.

VII. K.S.A. § 59-29a06

K.S.A. § 59-29a06 was enacted in 1994 and prior to the decision in Hendricks was amended only one time, post Hendricks the statute was amended five times. This part of the KSVPA is known as the Trial Counsel and Experts statute.

In the year 1995 the Kansas Legislature passed Senate Bill 3. Concerning this it changed that trial shall be held forty-five days after probable cause to sixty days after any hearing held under K.S.A. § 59-29a05. It added that the trial may be continued upon the request of either party or a showing of good cause, or by the court on its own motion in the due administration of justice, and when the Defendant will not be substantially prejudiced. Further, it granted the court(s) the discretion to determine if the person is or would be allowed an independent examination at the State's expense. This included the power to determine the amount of money to be spent.

In the year 1999 the Kansas Legislature passed House Bill 2102. Concerning this it added the following language: "A jury shall consist of 12 jurors unless the parties agree in writing with the approval of the court that the jury shall consist of any number of juror's less than 12 jurors. The person and the attorney general shall each have eight peremptory challenges, or in the case of a jury of less than 12 jurors, a proportionally equal number of peremptory challenges."

In the year 2003 the Kansas Legislature passed Senate Bill 27. Concerning this it added the following section: "(e) the provisions of this section are not jurisdictional, and failure to comply with such provisions in no way prevents the attorney general from proceeding against a person otherwise subject to the provision of K.S.A. 59-29a01 et seq., and amendments thereto."

In the year 2011 the Kansas Legislature passed House Bill 2071. Concerning this it added the following section: "(c) Notwithstanding K.S.A. 60-456, and amendments thereto, at any trial conducted under K.S.A. 59-29a01 et seq., and amendments thereto, the parties shall be permitted to call expert witnesses. The facts or data in the particular case upon which an expert bases an opinion or inference may be those perceived by or made known to the expert at or before the hearing. If the facts or data are of a type reasonably relied upon by experts in the particular field in forming opinions or inferences upon the subject, such facts and data need not be admissible in evidence in order for the opinion or inference to be admitted."

In the year 2012 the Kansas Legislature passed Senate Bill 280. Concerning this they made language changes that were non-consequential and did not affect any rights.

In the year 2015 the Kansas Legislature passed Senate Bill 12. Concerning this it changed the requirement that the Court will hold a trial within sixty days to where the court would set the matter for a pretrial conference to establish a mutually agreeable date for trial. It also changed that the person is entitled to an independent examiner and counsel at any proceeding under the KSVPA to where it is only applicable to a hearing held pursuant to this section of the KSVPA. In addition it added the following language: "Notwithstanding any other provision of law to the contrary, the provisions of this section relating to jury trials shall not apply to proceedings for annual review or proceedings on a petition for transitional release, conditional release or final discharge."

VIII. K.S.A. § 59-29a07

K.S.A. § 59-29a07 was enacted in 1994 and prior to the decision in Hendricks was amended only one time, post Hendricks the statute was amended seven times. This part of the KSVPA is known as the Commitment Procedure statute.

In the year 1995 the Kansas Legislature passed Senate Bill 3. It added the following language: "The Department of Social and Rehabilitation Services is authorized to enter into an interagency agreement with the department of corrections for the confinement of such persons. Such persons who are in the confinement of the secretary of corrections pursuant to an interagency agreement shall be segregated from any other person under the control and supervision housed and managed separately from offenders in the custody of the secretary of corrections, and except for occasional instances of supervised incidental contact, shall be segregated from such offenders."

Senate Bill 3 also added the following language: "Upon a mistrial, the court shall direct that the person be held at an appropriate secure facility, including, but not limited to, a county jail, until another trial is conducted. Any subsequent trial following a mistrial shall be held within 90 days of the previous trial, unless such subsequent trial is continued as provided in K.S.A. 59-29a06 and amendments thereto."

In the year 1999 the Kansas Legislature passed House Bill 2101. It added the following language: "If any person while committed to the custody of the secretary pursuant to this act shall be taken into custody by any law enforcement officer as defined in K.S.A. 21-3110 and amendments thereto pursuant to any parole revocation proceeding or any arrest or conviction for a criminal offense of any nature, upon the person's release from the custody of any law enforcement officer, the person shall be returned to the custody of the secretary for further treatment pursuant to this act. during any such period of time a person is not in the actual custody or supervision of the secretary, the secretary shall be excused from the provisions of K.S.A. 59-29a08 and amendments thereto, with regard to providing that person an annual examination, annual notice and annual report to the court, except that the secretary shall give notice to the court as soon as reasonably possible after the taking of the person into custody that the person is no longer in treatment pursuant to this act, and notice to the court when the person is returned to the custody of the secretary for further treatment."

In the year 2003 the Kansas Legislature passed Senate Bill 27. This only made grammatical changes to the statute.

In the year 2006 the Kansas Legislature passed Senate Bill 506. It added the following language: "The provisions of this subsection shall apply to any facility or building utilized in any transitional release program or conditional release program."

In the year 2011 the Kansas Legislature passed House Bill 2339. It made minor word changes due to the restructuring of the criminal procedure in Kansas, so that it correctly cites the correct statute.

In the year 2014 the Kansas Legislature passed Senate Bill 506. This amended K.S.A. § 59-29a07 Commitment Procedure. It changed the words "Department of Social and Rehabilitation Services" to "Kansas Department for Aging and Disability Services." This was done for the restructuring that had occurred in Kansas.

In the year 2015 the Kansas Legislature passed Senate Bill 12. This amended K.S.A. § 59-29a07 Commitment Procedure. It added that an appeal could be had in the manner provided for civil cases in Article 21 of Chapter 60 of the Kansas Statutes Annotated, and amendments thereto.

Senate Bill 12 also replaced the words: "K.S.A. 59-29a01 et. seq., and amendments thereto;" with the words: "The Kansas Sexually Violent Predator Act."

In the year 2018 the Kansas Legislature passed Senate Bill 266. It changed the terms of the statute to where the secure confinement restriction shall not apply to reintegration, transition, or conditional release facilities or buildings.

IX. K.S.A. § 59-29a08

K.S.A. § 59-29a08 was enacted in 1994 and prior to the decision in Hendricks was amended only one time, post Hendricks the statute was amended seven times. This part of the KSVPA is known as the Annual Review statute.

In the year 1998 the Kansas Legislature passed Senate Bill 671. The Legislature added a paragraph requiring the individual, if Court ordered to transition, to comply with any rules or regulations the secretary may establish for this program and every directive of the treatment staff of the transitional release program. It also gave jurisdiction to the Court and the State to place one back in secure confinement if they violated any rule, regulation or directive associated with the transitional release pro-

SEXUALLY VIOLENT OFFENDER

gram. It also provided for a provision that allowed for the move back to secure confinement to occur before any hearing is held or Due Process is provided.

In the year 2003 the Kansas Legislature passed Senate Bill 27. The amendment required that the secretary shall provide the committed person with an annual written notice of the person's right to petition the court for release over the secretary's objection. The notice shall contain a waiver of rights. The secretary shall also forward the annual report, as well as the annual notice and waiver form, to the court that committed the person under K.S.A. 59-29a01 et seq., and amendments thereto. It also made a state created liberty interest that the committed individual shall not be denied from seeking full discharge during an annual review.

In the year 2007 the Kansas Legislature passed Senate Bill 52. It gave jurisdiction to the Court to hold a review hearing when there is current evidence from an expert or professional person that an identified physiological change to the committed person, such as paralysis, stroke or dementia, that renders the committed person unable to commit a sexually violent offense and this change is permanent; and the evidence presents a change in condition since the person's last hearing.

In the year 2015 the Kansas Legislature passed Senate Bill 12. This amendment repealed the amendment made in Senate Bill 52 (2007). It also removed the ability to have a jury trial during an annual review hearing. Instead now all must be heard to the bench.

In the year 2017 the Kansas Legislature passed House Bill 2128. The amendment set that the committed person is required to file a request for annual review within forty-five (45) days of the date the Secretary files the annual report or forego the constitutional rights during an annual review (i.e. counsel, hearing, etc.). Requiring only an in camera inspection if no petition for review filed.

House Bill 2128 also set a requirement that one in secure confinement could only petition for transitional release, one in transitional release could petition for conditional release and one in conditional release could petition for full discharge.

House Bill 2128 placed the burden to show probable cause on the person committed and set a standard that if the committed person is not participating in treatment it is presumed that he will be unable to show probable cause and thus recommitment can be automatic.

In the year 2018 the Kansas Legislature passed Senate Bill 266. The amendment set forth a requirement that the Court shall provide a file-stamped copy of the report filed by the Secretary to the Attorney General and requiring the Attorney General to forward a copy to the Secretary upon receipt.

Senate Bill 266 also set that conditional release shall be a minimum of five (5) years and requires the person be free of violations of conditions of such person's treatment plan for said five (5) years in order to gain release or full discharge.

X. K.S.A. § 59-29a09

K.S.A. § 59-29a09 was enacted in 1994 and has had no amendments or changes made to it since it was put in place. This statute sets that Constitutional requirements shall be followed.

XI. K.S.A. § 59-29a10

K.S.A. § 59-29a10 was enacted in 1994 and prior to the decision in Hendricks was amended only one time, post Hendricks the statute was amended four times. This part of the KSVPA is known as the Transitional Release statute.

In the year 1995 the Kansas Legislature passed Senate Bill 3. It switched the wording from county or district attorney to attorney general.

In the year 1998 the Kansas Legislature passed Senate Bill 671. It added two new sections to the statute as follows: (b) If after the hearing the court is convinced beyond a reasonable doubt that the person is not appropriate for transitional release, the court shall order that the person remain in secure commitment. Otherwise, the court shall order that the person be placed in transitional release. (c) The provisions of subsections (d), (e) and (f) of K S.A. 59-29a08 and amendments thereto shall apply to a transitional release pursuant to this section.

In the year 2003 the Kansas Legislature passed Senate Bill 27. It made grammatical and word substitutions to the statute.

In the year 2015 the Kansas Legislature passed Senate Bill 12. It made grammatical and word substitutions to the statute.

In the year 2017 the Kansas Legislature passed House Bill 2128. It made grammatical and word substitutions to the statute. It also added one new section, with three subsections, to the statute as follows: (b) (1) If the secretary determines that the person's mental abnormality or personality disorder has significantly changed so that the person is not likely to engage in repeat acts of sexual violence if placed in conditional release, the secretary shall authorize the person to petition the court for conditional release. The petition shall be served upon the court and the attorney general. The court, upon service of the petition for conditional release, shall issue notice of a hearing to be scheduled within 30 days. The attorney general shall represent the state, and shall have the right to have the Plaintiff examined by an expert or professional person of the attorney general's choice. The burden of proof shall be upon the attorney general to show beyond a reasonable doubt that the Plaintiff's mental abnormality or personality disorder remains such that the Plaintiff is not safe to be at large and that if placed in conditional release is likely to engage in repeat acts of sexual violence. (2) If, after the hearing, the court is convinced beyond a reasonable doubt that the person is not sufficiently safe to warrant conditional release, the court shall order that the person remain either in secure commitment or in transitional release. Otherwise, the court shall order that the person be placed in conditional release. (3) The provisions of K.S.A. 59-29a18(h) and 59-29a19(a) (d) and (e), and amendments thereto, shall apply to a conditional release pursuant to this section.

XII. K.S.A. § 59-29a11

K.S.A. § 59-29a11 was enacted in 1994 and prior to the decision in Hendricks was never amended, post Hendricks the statute was amended seven times. This part of the KSVPA is known as the Forms of Release statute.

In the year 1998 the Kansas Legislature passed Senate Bill 671. It made grammatical and word substitutions to the statute.

In the year 2006 the Kansas Legislature passed Senate Bill 506. It added two new sections to the statute as follows: (b) No transitional release or conditional release facility or building shall be located within 2,000 feet of a licensed child care facility, registered family day care home, an established place of worship, any residence in which a child under 18 years of age resides, or the real property of any school upon which is located a structure used by a unified school district or an accredited nonpublic school for student instruction or attendance or extracurricular activities of pupils enrolled in kindergarten or any grades one through 12. This subsection shall not apply to any state correctional institution or facility. (c) Transitional release or conditional release facilities or buildings shall be subject to all regulations applicable to other property and buildings located in the zone or area that are imposed by any municipality through zoning ordinance, resolution or regulation, such municipality's building regulatory codes, subdivision regulations or other nondiscriminatory regulations.

In the year 2009 the Kansas Legislature passed Senate Bill 91. It added two new sections to the statute as follows: (d) On and after January 1, 2009, the secretary of social and rehabilitation services shall place no more than eight sexually violent predators in any one county on transitional release or conditional release. (e) The secretary of social and rehabilitation services shall submit an annual report to the governor and the legislature during the first week of the regular legislative session detailing activities related to the transitional release and conditional release of sexually violent predators. the report shall include the status of such predators who have been placed in transitional release or conditional release including the number of any such predators and their locations; information regarding the number of predators who have been returned to the sexually violent predator treatment program at Larned State Hospital along with the reasons for such return; and any plans for the development of additional transitional release or conditional release facilities.

In the year 2010 the Kansas Legislature passed Senate Bill 91. The amendment removed the words, "registered family day care home."

In the year 2014 the Kansas Legislature passed House Bill 2515. The amendment changed the words for the change in custody from SRS to KDADS.

In the year 2015 the Kansas Legislature passed Senate Bill 12. It made grammatical and word substitutions to the statute. Most notable is that on and after July 1, 2015, sixteen can be in one county on transition or conditional release.

In the year 2018 the Kansas Legislature passed Senate Bill 266. The amendment removed the limit on the number of persons in any one county while on conditional release.

XIII. K.S.A. § 59-29a12

K.S.A. § 59-29a12 was enacted in 1994 and prior to the decision in Hendricks was never amended, post Hendricks the statute was amended two times. This part of the KSVPA is known as the Costs statute.

In the year 1998 the Kansas Legislature passed Senate Bill 671. The amendment removed the words "of social and rehabilitation services."

In the year 2007 the Kansas Legislature passed Senate Bill 52. The amendment instituted an entirely new statute that reads as follows: (a) For state budgetary purposes, the secretary shall be responsible for all cost relating to the evaluation and treatment of persons committed to the secretary's custody under any provision of this act. Payment for the maintenance, care and treatment of any such committed person shall be paid by the person, by the conservator of such person's estate or by any person bound by law to support such person. Reimbursement may be obtained by the secretary for the cost of care and treatment, including placement in transitional release, of persons committed to the secretary's custody pursuant to K.S.A. 59-2006, and amendments thereto. (b) When court orders a person committed to the secretary's custody under any provision of this act to appear at a court proceeding, the county where such court is located shall be responsible for the transportation, security and control of such person and all costs involved. The secretary shall not be required to provide an employee to travel with the committed person. (c) Except as provided further, when a court proceeding is initiated by the committed person, such person shall be responsible for making all arrangements concerning the transportation, security and control of such person and all costs involved. The secretary shall review and approve all arrangements prior to the court proceeding. The secretary may deny the arrangements if such arrangements fail to meet security standards. The provisions of this subsection shall not apply to a hearing pursuant to K.S.A. 59-29a08, and amendments thereto. (d) The secretary shall adopt rules and regulations to implement this section.

XIV. K.S.A. § 59-29a13

K.S.A. § 59-29a13 was enacted in 1994 and prior to the decision in

Hendricks was never amended, post Hendricks the statute was amended one time. This part of the KSVPA is known as the Victim Notification statute.

In the year 1998 the Kansas Legislature passed Senate Bill 671. It made grammatical and word substitutions to the statute.

XV. K.S.A. § 59-29a14

K.S.A. § 59-29a14 was enacted in 1994 and prior to the decision in Hendricks was never amended, post Hendricks the statute was amended three times. This part of the KSVPA is known as the Costs statute.

In the year 2010 the Kansas Legislature passed House Bill 2656. The amendment changed from 10 days to 14 days.

In the year 2011 the Kansas Legislature passed House Bill 2339. The amendment made grammatical and word substitutions to the statute.

In the year 2015 the Kansas Legislature passed Senate Bill 113. Due to the change to the criminal code in Kansas the reference to criminal statutes was changed to list the new numbers.

XVI. K.S.A. § 59-29a15

K.S.A. § 59-29a15 was enacted in 1994 and has had no amendments or changes made to it since it was put in place. This the severability clause for the KSVPA.

XVII. K.S.A. § 59-29a16

K.S.A. § 59-29a16 was enacted in 1995 and has had no amendments or changes made to it since it was put in place. This is the statute concerning privileged information and records for the KSVPA.

XVIII. K.S.A. § 59-29a17

K.S.A. § 59-29a17 was enacted in 1995 and has had no amendments or changes made to it since it was put in place. This is the statute concerning court records and the sealing thereof.

XIX. K.S.A. § 59-29a18

K.S.A. § 59-29a18 was enacted in 1998 and prior to the decision in Hendricks was never amended, post Hendricks the statute was amended four times. This part of the KSVPA is known as the Conditional Release statute.

The Legislature added a new section to the KSVPA, K.S.A. § 59-29a18, in the year 1998 (Senate Bill 671). It set forth a procedure whereby the committed person could be released to conditional release. It set that conditional release shall be a minimum of five years in length. Defined and set a procedure for a hearing to determine eligibility for conditional release.

In the year 1999 the Kansas Legislature passed House Bill 2101. The amendment made grammatical and word substitutions to the statute.

In the year 2015 the Kansas Legislature passed Senate Bill 12. The amendment repealed the entire statute and removed it from the law books.

In the year 2016 the Kansas Legislature passed Senate Bill 407. The amendment re-created K.S.A. § 59-29a18.

In the year 2017 the Kansas Legislature passed House Bill 2128. The amendment replaced the entire statute with a new statute.

XX. K.S.A. § 59-29a19

K.S.A. § 59-29a19 was enacted in 1998 and prior to the decision in Hendricks was never amended, post Hendricks the statute was amended three times. This part of the KSVPA is known as the Conditional Release Specifics statute.

The Legislature added a new section to the KSVPA, K.S.A. § 59-29a19, in the year 1998 (Senate Bill 671). The amendment defined the term "conditional release," what the procedure was for a person being placed on it, and set a Due Process procedure in place that was mandatory if the State wished to revoke this release. It also set the period of conditional release was to be no less than a minimum of five (5) years.

In the year 1999 the Kansas Legislature passed House Bill 2101. The amendment made grammatical and word substitutions to the statute.

In the year 2010 the Kansas Legislature passed House Bill 2195. The amendment made grammatical and word substitutions to the statute.

In the year 2018 the Kansas Legislature passed Senate Bill 266. The amendment added that the Progress Review Panel had the authority to assist in developing the treatment plan for one on conditional release. It set forth that conditions of conditional release shall include: "Having no direct contact with individuals that match the person's victim template, travel restrictions, searches, home visits, substance abuse testing and registration requirements;" setting forth what a conditional release monitor is and what authority they have; and setting forth that the person must have five years without any violations of conditions of such person's treatment plan, the treatment staff, or other treatment providers, in order to be eligible for release from conditional release.

XXI. K.S.A. § 59-29a20

K.S.A. § 59-29a20 was enacted in 1999 and has had no amendments or changes made to it since it was put in place. This is the statute concerning pre-trial release for one being tried as a Sexually Violent Predator.

XXII. K.S.A. § 59-29a21

K.S.A. § 59-29a21 was enacted in 2003 and has had no amendments or changes made to it since it was put in place. This is another statute concerning severability.

XXIII. K.S.A. § 59-29a22

K.S.A. § 59-29a22 was enacted in 2007 and prior to the decision in Hendricks was never amended, post Hendricks the statute was amended three times. This part of the KSVPA is known as the Bill of Rights statute.

The Legislature added a new section to the KSVPA, K.S.A. § 59-29a22, in the year 2007 (Senate Bill 52). This created a Bill of rights for SVP's enforceable through the Court. Through Judicial review it was found to have created several liberty interests. Included in these rights, only partially listed not meant to be all inclusive, was:

The right to mail;

The right to no forced treatment;

The right to no seclusion;

The right to no forced medication;

The right to property;

The right to privacy;

The right to an adequate administrative remedy;

The right to telephonic communication; and

A definition and outline of the necessary and mandatory process to be used to strip deny or restrict any of these rights, which was limited to only seven of the rights enumerated.

In the year 2014 the Kansas Legislature passed House Bill 2515. This allowed the Department of Social and Rehabilitation Services to be removed and replaced with the Kansas Department on Aging and Disability Services who was given control of the SPTP, therefore, it was just a language change substituting one agency for the other.

In the year 2015 the Kansas Legislature passed Senate Bill 12. This amendment made sweeping changes, such as:

The word patient was changed to person;

It created and enacted an "emergency lockdown" procedure;

It created and enacted an "Individual person Management Plan (IPMP)" procedure. This allows for seclusion based on a specific procedure;

It changed from "…shall have the following rights:" to "… shall have the following statutory rights;"

Changed the rules concerning the right to refuse medication for medical or psychiatric reasons or purposes;

Creation of the ability of KDADS to place the person committed in locked isolation during transport or while in another health care or treatment facility;

Changing the right to individual religion and worship. Now said practice must comply with the applicable laws and rules of the facility;

Concerning the right to inspect and receive a copy of records in custody of the facility, requires the person to pay for them and allows for the denial of access by the head of the facility;

Removal that all incoming or outgoing mail may be inspected if there is reason to believe it contains contraband. The change made it to where they may inspect any incoming or outgoing mail at any time;

Adding a statement that the person shall not be allowed to receive sexually explicit material, items that jeopardize their treatment or treatment of others and that may affect the therapeutic environment. The legislature delegated the authority to define this to KDADS;

A change to the right to keep and wear one's own clothing. This amendment makes it a requirement that it complies to the rules set forth by KDADS in order for the person to have the right;

A change to the right to keep and use one's personal property. This amendment makes it a requirement that it complies to the rules set forth by KDADS in order for the person to have the right;

A change to the right to spend one's own money as they choose. This now requires that it only be allowed if done in compliance with the rules set forth by KDADS;

Adding a section that KDADS may enact any rule as long as it applies to all equally, at which time the person is not entitled to Due Process or any form of review, they are only to be notified;

Adding a new set of steps to the administrative review policy. Now one must abide by the Kansas Administrative Procedure Act and Kansas Judicial Review Act. In addition said proceeding must be heard by and through the Office of Administrative Hearings before it can be deemed exhausted; and

Designates Pawnee County Court as the only Court with jurisdiction to hear any case brought under the Kansas Judicial review Act.

In the year 2018 the Kansas Legislature passed Senate Bill 266. This made two changes to the statute: (1) A change to what is allowed under the IPMP; and (2) Granting the Office of Administrative hearings a mandatory requirement to dismiss any hearing request if it cannot be shown that administrative remedies at the facility were exhausted by the person.

XXIV. K.S.A. § 59-29a23

K.S.A. § 59-29a23 was enacted in 2011 and prior to the decision in Hendricks was never amended, post Hendricks the statute was amended one time. This part of the KSVPA is known as the Habeas Corpus Rules statute.

The Legislature added a new section to the KSVPA, K.S.A. § 59-29a23, in the year 2011 (House Bill 2071). The new statute required the county that committed the SVP to pay all costs associated when the SVP filed a Writ of Habeas Corpus Petition, including but not limited to costs of appointed counsel fees and expenses, witness fees and expenses, expert fees and expenses, and other expenses related to the prosecution and defense of such petition.

In the year 2015 the Kansas Legislature passed Senate Bill 12. This set that the SVP shall be required to pay the full filing fee of any legal action.

XXV. K.S.A. § 59-29a24

K.S.A. § 59-29a24 was enacted in 2012 and prior to the decision in Hendricks was never amended, post Hendricks the statute was amended one time. This part of the KSVPA is known as the Civil Actions statute.

The Legislature added a new section to the KSVPA, K.S.A. § 59-29a24, in the year 2012 (Senate Bill 74). This set a requirement that a committed SVP must exhaust administrative remedies before filing a legal action in court. It also added a three strikes provision for habitual filers.

In the year 2015 the Kansas Legislature passed Senate Bill 12. This amendment removed the three strikes provision, but still required exhaustion of administrative remedies prior to filing.

XXVI. K.S.A. § 59-29a24a

K.S.A. § 59-29a24a was enacted in 2015 and repealed in 2016. During its existence it was similar to K.S.A. § 59-29a24.

XXVII. K.S.A. § 59-29a25

K.S.A. § 59-29a25 was enacted in 2015 and has had no amendments or changes made to it since it was put in place. This statute concerns what to do when an SVP suffers a permanent physiological change.

XXVIII. K.S.A. § 59-29a26

K.S.A. § 59-29a26 was enacted in 2015 and has had no amendments or changes made to it since it was put in place. This is the statute setting that the county is responsible for the costs.

XXIX. K.S.A. § 59-29a27

K.S.A. § 59-29a27 was enacted in 2015 and has had no amendments or changes made to it since it was put in place. This sets who has the duty of care for an SVP who has pending criminal charges.

CHAPTER 4

STATUTES THAT COMPRISE THE KSVPA

———————❧———————

K.S.A. 59-29a01. Commitment of sexually violent predators; legislative findings; time requirements directory.

(a) The legislature finds that there exists an extremely dangerous group of sexually violent predators who have a mental abnormality or personality disorder and who are likely to engage in repeat acts of sexual violence if not treated for their mental abnormality or personality disorder. Because the existing civil commitment procedures under K.S.A. 59-2901 et seq., and amendments thereto, are inadequate to address the special needs of sexually violent predators and the risks they present to society, the legislature determines that a separate involuntary civil commitment process for the potentially long-term control, care and treatment of sexually violent predators is necessary. The legislature also determines that because of the nature of the mental abnormalities or personality disorders from which sexually violent predators suffer and the dangers they present, it is necessary to house involuntarily committed sexually violent predators in an environment separate from persons involuntarily committed under K.S.A. 59-2901 et seq., and amendments thereto.

(b) Notwithstanding any other evidence of legislative intent, it is hereby declared that any time requirements set forth in K.S.A. 59-29a01 et seq., and amendments thereto, either as originally enacted or as amended, are intended to be directory and not mandatory and serve as guidelines for conducting proceedings under K.S.A. 59-29a01 et seq., and amendments thereto.

(c) The provisions of K.S.A. 59-29a01 et seq., and amendments thereto, shall be known and may be cited as the Kansas sexually violent predator act.

K.S.A. 59-29a02. Commitment of sexually violent predators; definitions.

As used in this act:

(a) "Sexually violent predator" means any person who has been convicted of or charged with a sexually violent offense and who suffers from a mental abnormality or personality disorder which makes the person likely to engage in repeat acts of sexual violence and who has serious difficulty in controlling such person's dangerous behavior.

(b) "Mental abnormality" means a congenital or acquired condition affecting the emotional or volitional capacity which predisposes the person to commit sexually violent offenses in a degree constituting such person a menace to the health and safety of others.

(c) "Likely to engage in repeat acts of sexual violence" means the person's propensity to commit acts of sexual violence is of such a degree as to pose a menace to the health and safety of others.

(d) "Sexually motivated" means that one of the purposes for which the defendant committed the crime was for the purpose of the defendant's sexual gratification.

(e) "Sexually violent offense" means:

(1) Rape, as defined in K.S.A. 21-3502, prior to its repeal, or K.S.A. 2017 Supp. 21-5503, and amendments thereto;

(2) Indecent liberties with a child, as defined in K.S.A. 21-3503, prior to its repeal, or K.S.A. 2017 Supp. 21-5506(a), and amendments thereto;

(3) Aggravated indecent liberties with a child, as defined in K.S.A. 21-3504, prior to its repeal, or K.S.A. 2017 Supp. 21-5506(b), and amend-

ments thereto;

(4) Criminal sodomy, as defined in K.S.A. 21-3505(a)(2) and (a)(3), prior to its repeal, or K.S.A. 2017 Supp. 21-5504(a)(3) and (a)(4), and amendments thereto;

(5) Aggravated criminal sodomy, as defined in K.S.A. 21-3506, prior to its repeal, or K.S.A. 2017 Supp. 21-5504(b), and amendments thereto;

(6) Indecent solicitation of a child, as defined in K.S.A. 21-3510, prior to its repeal, or K.S.A. 2017 Supp. 21-5508(a), and amendments thereto;

(7) Aggravated indecent solicitation of a child, as defined in K.S.A. 21-3511, prior to its repeal, or K.S.A. 2017 Supp. 21-5508(b), and amendments thereto;

(8) Sexual exploitation of a child, as defined in K.S.A. 21-3516, prior to its repeal, or K.S.A. 2017 Supp. 21-5510, and amendments thereto;

(9) Aggravated sexual battery, as defined in K.S.A. 21-3518, prior to its repeal, or K.S.A. 2017 Supp. 21-5505(b), and amendments thereto;

(10) Aggravated incest, as defined in K.S.A. 21-3603, prior to its repeal, or K.S.A. 2017 Supp. 21-5604(b), and amendments thereto;

(11) Any conviction for a felony offense in effect at any time prior to the effective date of this act, that is comparable to a sexually violent offense as defined in paragraphs (1) through (11) or any federal or other state conviction for a felony offense that under the laws of this state would be a sexually violent offense as defined in this section;

(12) An attempt, conspiracy or criminal solicitation, as defined in K.S.A. 21-3301, 21-3302 and 21-3303, prior to their repeal, or K.S.A. 2017 Supp. 21-5301, 21-5302 or 21-5303, and amendments thereto, of a sexually violent offense as defined in this subsection; or

(13) Any act which either at the time of sentencing for the offense or subsequently during civil commitment proceedings pursuant to this act, has been determined beyond a reasonable doubt to have been sexually motivated.

(f) "Agency with jurisdiction" means that agency which releases upon lawful order or authority a person serving a sentence or term of confinement and includes the department of corrections, the Kansas department for aging and disability services and the prisoner review board.

(g) "Person" means an individual who is a potential or actual subject of proceedings under this act.

(h) "Treatment staff" means the persons, agencies or firms employed by or contracted with the secretary to provide treatment, supervision or other services at the sexually violent predator facility.

(i) "Transitional release" means any halfway house, work release, sexually violent predator treatment facility or other placement designed to assist the person's adjustment and reintegration into the community.

(j) "Secretary" means the secretary for aging and disability services.

(k) "Conditional release" means approved placement in the community for a minimum of five years while under the supervision of the person's court of original commitment and monitored by the secretary for aging and disability services.

(l) "Conditional release monitor" means an individual appointed by the court to monitor the person's compliance with the treatment plan while placed on conditional release and who reports to the court. Such monitor shall not be a court services officer.

(m) "Progress review panel" means individuals appointed by the secretary for aging and disability services to evaluate a person's progress in the sexually violent predator treatment program.

K.S.A. 59-29a03. Same; notice of release of sexually violent predator by agency with jurisdiction to attorney general and multidisciplinary team, time, contents; immunity from liability; establishing a multidisciplinary team; appointment of a prosecutor's review committee; assessment of person; provisions of section are not jurisdictional.

(a) When it appears that a person may meet the criteria of a sexually violent predator as defined in K.S.A. 59-29a02, and amendments thereto, the agency with jurisdiction shall give written notice of such to the attorney general and the multidisciplinary team established in subsection (f), 90 days prior to:

(1) The anticipated release from total confinement of a person who has been convicted of a sexually violent offense, except that in the case of persons who are returned to prison for no more than 90 days as a result of revocation of postrelease supervision, written notice shall be given as soon as practicable following the person's readmission to prison;

(2) Release of a person who has been charged with a sexually violent offense and who has been determined to be incompetent to stand trial pursuant to K.S.A. 22-3305, and amendments thereto;

(3) Release of a person who has been found not guilty by reason of insanity of a sexually violent offense pursuant to K.S.A. 22-3428, and

amendments thereto; or

(4) Release of a person who has been found not guilty of a sexually violent offense pursuant to K.S.A. 22-3428, and amendments thereto, and the jury who returned the verdict of not guilty answers in the affirmative to the special question asked pursuant to K.S.A. 22-3221, and amendments thereto.

(b) The agency with jurisdiction shall inform the attorney general and the multidisciplinary team established in subsection (f) of the following:

(1) The person's name, identifying factors, anticipated future residence and offense history; and

(2) Documentation of institutional adjustment and any treatment received.

(c) Any reports of evaluations prepared or provided pursuant to subsection (b) shall demonstrate that the person evaluated was informed of the following:(1) The nature and purpose of the evaluation; and (2) that the evaluation will not be confidential and that any statements made by the person and any conclusions drawn by the evaluator may be disclosed to a court, the detained person's attorney, the prosecutor and the trier of fact at any proceeding conducted under the Kansas sexually violent predator act.

(d) The permitted disclosures required to be submitted to the attorney general under this section shall be deemed to be in response to the attorney general's civil demand for relevant and material information to investigate whether a petition shall be filed. The information provided shall be specific to the purposes of the Kansas sexually violent predator act and as limited in scope as reasonably practicable.

(e) The agency with jurisdiction, its employees, officials, members of the multidisciplinary team established in subsection (f), members of the prosecutor's review committee appointed as provided in subsection (g) and individuals contracting, appointed or volunteering to perform services hereunder shall be immune from liability for any good-faith conduct under this section.

(f) The secretary of corrections shall establish a multidisciplinary team which may include individuals from other state agencies to review available records of each person referred to such team pursuant to subsection (a). The team shall include the mental health professional who prepared any evaluation, interviewed the person or made any recommendation to the attorney general. The team shall assess whether or not the person meets the definition of a sexually violent predator, as established in K.S.A. 59-29a02, and amendments thereto. The team shall notify the attorney general of its assessment.

(g) The attorney general shall appoint a prosecutor's review committee to review the records of each person referred to the attorney general pursuant to subsection (a). The prosecutor's review committee shall assist the attorney general in the determination of whether or not the person meets the definition of a sexually violent predator. The assessment of the multidisciplinary team shall be made available to the attorney general and the prosecutor's review committee.

(h) The provisions of this section are not jurisdictional and failure to comply with such provisions not affecting constitutional rights in no way prevents the attorney general from proceeding against a person otherwise subject to the provisions of the Kansas sexually violent predator act.

K.S.A. 59-29a04. Same; petition, time, contents; provisions of section are not jurisdictional; county reimbursed for costs.

(a) When the prosecutor's review committee, appointed as provided in K.S.A. 59-29a03(g), and amendments thereto, has determined that the person meets the definition of a sexually violent predator, the attorney general, within 75 days of the date the attorney general received the written notice as provided in K.S.A. 59-29a03(a), and amendments thereto, may file a petition in the county where the person was convicted of or charged with a sexually violent offense alleging that the person is a sexually violent predator and stating sufficient facts to support such allegation.

(b) Notwithstanding the provisions of subsection (a), when the person named in the petition is a person who has been convicted of or charged with a federal or other state offense that under the laws of this state would be a sexually violent offense, as defined in K.S.A. 59-29a02, and amendments thereto, the attorney general may file the petition in the county where the person now resides, was charged or convicted of any offense, or was released.

(c) Service of the petition on the attorney appointed or hired to represent the person shall be deemed sufficient service.

(d) The provisions of this section are not jurisdictional, and failure to comply with such provisions not affecting constitutional rights in no way prevents the attorney general from proceeding against a person otherwise subject to the provisions of the Kansas sexually violent predator act.

(e) Whenever a determination is made regarding whether a person may be a sexually violent predator, the county responsible for the costs incurred, including, but not limited to, costs of investigation, prosecution, defense, juries, witness fees and expenses, expert fees and expenses and other expenses related to determining whether a person may be a sexually violent predator, shall be reimbursed for such costs by the office of the attorney general from the sexually violent predator expense fund. The attorney general shall develop and implement a procedure to provide such reimbursements. If there are no moneys available in such fund to pay any such reimbursements, the county may file a claim against the state pursuant to article 9 of chapter 46, of the Kansas Statutes Annotated, and amendments thereto.

(f) The person against whom a petition is filed shall be responsible for the costs of the medical care and treatment provided or made accessible by the governmental entity having custody, and the governmental entity having custody may seek reimbursement from the person against whom a petition has been filed for such costs.

(g) Pre-commitment proceedings, post-commitment proceedings, including conditional release and final discharge and other court proceedings are civil in nature. Such proceedings shall follow the procedures set forth in chapter 60 of the Kansas Statutes Annotated, and amendments thereto, except as expressly provided elsewhere in the Kansas sexually violent predator act.

K.S.A. 59-29a04a. Sexually violent predator expense fund.

(a) There is hereby created in the state treasury the sexually violent predator expense fund which shall be administered by the attorney general. All moneys credited to such fund shall be used to reimburse counties under:

(1) K.S.A. 59-29a04, and amendments thereto, responsible for the costs related to determining whether a person may be a sexually violent predator; and

(2) K.S.A. 2014 Supp. 59-29a23, and amendments thereto, for the costs related to a person filing a civil action relating to the civil commitment pursuant to the Kansas sexually violent predator act.

(b) All expenditures from the sexually violent predator expense fund shall be made in accordance with appropriation acts upon warrants of the director of accounts and reports issued pursuant to vouchers approved by the attorney general or the attorney general's designee.

K.S.A. 59-29a05. Same; determination of probable cause, hearing; evaluation; person taken into custody.

(a) Upon filing of a petition under K.S.A. 59-29a04, and amendments thereto, the judge shall determine whether probable cause exists to believe that the person named in the petition is a sexually violent predator. If such determination is made, the judge shall:

(1) Direct that person be taken into custody and detained in the county jail until such time as a determination is made that the person is a sexually violent predator subject to commitment under the Kansas sexually violent predator act; and

(2) File a protective order permitting disclosures of protected health information to the parties, their counsel, evaluators, experts and others necessary to the litigation during the course of the proceedings subject to the Kansas sexually violent predator act.

(b) Within 72 hours after a person is taken into custody pursuant to subsection (a), or as soon as reasonably practicable or agreed upon by the parties, such person shall be provided with notice of, and an opportunity to appear in person at, a hearing to contest probable cause as to whether the detained person is a sexually violent predator. At this hearing the court shall: (1) Verify the detainer's identity; and (2) determine whether probable cause exists to believe that the person is a sexually violent predator. The state may rely upon the petition and supplement the petition with additional documentary evidence or live testimony.

(c) At the probable cause hearing as provided in subsection (b), the detained person shall have the following rights in addition to the rights previously specified: (1) To be represented by counsel; (2) to present evidence on such person's behalf; (3) to cross-examine witnesses who testify against such person; and (4) to view and copy all petitions and reports in the court file.

(d) If the probable cause determination is made, the court shall order that the person be transferred to an appropriate secure facility, including, but not limited to, a county jail, for an evaluation as to whether the person is a sexually violent predator. The evaluation ordered by the court shall be conducted by a person deemed to be professionally qualified to conduct such an examination.

(e) The person conducting the evaluation ordered by the court pursuant to this section shall notify the detained person of the following: (1) The nature and purpose of the evaluation; and (2) that the evaluation will not be confidential and that any statements made by the detained person and any conclusions drawn by the evaluator, will be disclosed to the court, the detained person's attorney, the prosecutor and the trier of fact at any proceeding conducted under the Kansas sexually violent predator act.

K.S.A. 59-29a06. Same; trial; counsel and experts; indigent persons; jury, composition, peremptory challenges; provisions not jurisdictional.

(a) Within 60 days after the completion of any hearing held pursuant to K.S.A. 59-29a05, and amendments thereto, the court shall set the matter for a pretrial conference to establish a mutually agreeable date for trial to determine whether the person is a sexually violent predator. The trial may be continued upon the request of either party and a showing of good cause, or by the court on its own motion in the due administration of justice and when the respondent will not be substantially prejudiced.

(b) In proceedings under this section, the person shall be entitled to the assistance of counsel and an independent examination pursuant to K.S.A. 60-235, and amendments thereto, and if the person is indigent, the court shall appoint counsel to assist such person. When the person wishes to be examined pursuant to K.S.A. 60-235, and amendments thereto, the examiner shall be permitted to have reasonable access to the person for the purpose of such examination, as well as to all relevant medical and psychological records and reports. In the case of a person who is indigent, the court, upon the person's request, shall determine whether the services are necessary and reasonable compensation for such services. If the court determines that the services are necessary and the examiner's requested compensation for such services is reasonable, the court shall assist the person in obtaining an examiner to perform an examination or participate in the trial on the person's behalf. The court shall approve payment for such services upon the filing of a certified claim for compensation supported by a written statement specifying the time expended, services rendered, expenses incurred on behalf of the person and compensation received in the same case or for the same services from any other source.

(c) Notwithstanding K.S.A. 60-456, and amendments thereto, at any proceeding conducted under the Kansas sexually violent predator act, the parties shall be permitted to call expert witnesses. The facts or data in the particular case upon which an expert bases an opinion or inference may be those perceived by or made known to the expert at or before the hearing. If the facts or data are of a type reasonably relied upon by experts in the particular field in forming opinions or inferences upon the subject, such facts and data need not be admissible in evidence in order for the opinion or inference to be admitted.

(d) The person, the attorney general, or the judge shall have the right to demand that the trial be before a jury. Such demand for the trial to be before a jury shall be filed, in writing, at least four days prior to trial. Number and selection of jurors shall be determined as provided in K.S.A. 22-3403, and amendments thereto. If no demand is made, the trial shall be before the court.

(e) A jury shall consist of 12 jurors unless the parties agree in writing with the approval of the court that the jury shall consist of any number of jurors less than 12 jurors. The person and the attorney general shall each have eight peremptory challenges, or in the case of a jury of less than 12 jurors, a proportionally equal number of peremptory challenges.

(f) Notwithstanding any other provision of law to the contrary, the provisions of this section relating to jury trials shall not apply to proceedings for annual review or proceedings on a petition for transitional release, conditional release or final discharge.

K.S.A. 59-29a07. Same; determination; commitment procedure; interagency agreements; mistrials; persons committed and later taken into custody after parole, arrest or conviction, procedure; persons found incompetent to stand trial, procedure.

(a) The court or jury shall determine whether, beyond a reasonable doubt, the person is a sexually violent predator. If such determination that the person is a sexually violent predator is made by a jury, such determination shall be by unanimous verdict of such jury. Such determination may be appealed in the manner provided for civil cases in article 21 of chapter 60 of the Kansas Statutes Annotated, and amendments thereto. If the court or jury determines that the person is a sexually violent predator, the person shall be committed to the custody of the secretary for aging and disability services for control, care and treatment until such time as the person's mental abnormality or personality disorder has so changed that the person is safe to be at large. Such control, care and treatment shall be provided at a facility operated by the Kansas department for aging and disability services.

(b) At all times, persons committed for control, care and treatment by the Kansas department for aging and disability services pursuant to the Kansas sexually violent predator act shall be kept in a secure facility and such persons shall be segregated on different units from any other patient under the supervision of the secretary for aging and disability services and commencing June 1, 1995, such persons committed pursuant to the Kansas sexually violent predator act shall be kept in a facility or building separate from any other patient under the supervision of the secretary. The secure confinement restriction shall not apply to any reintegration, transitional release or conditional release facility or building.

(c) The Kansas department for aging and disability services is authorized to enter into an interagency agreement with the department of corrections for the confinement of such persons. Such persons who are in the confinement of the secretary of corrections pursuant to an interagency agreement shall be housed and managed separately from offenders in the custody of the secretary of corrections, and except for occasional instances of supervised incidental contact, shall be segregated from such offenders.

(d) If any person while committed to the custody of the secretary pursuant to the Kansas sexually violent predator act shall be taken into custody by any law enforcement officer as defined in K.S.A. 2017 Supp. 21-5111, and amendments thereto, pursuant to any parole revocation proceeding or any arrest or conviction for a criminal offense of any nature, upon the person's release from the custody of any law enforcement officer, the person shall be returned to the custody of the secretary for further treatment pursuant to the Kansas sexually violent predator act. During any such period of time a person is not in the actual custody or supervision of the secretary, the secretary shall be excused from the provisions of K.S.A. 59-29a08, and amendments thereto, with regard to providing that person an annual examination, annual notice and annual report to the court, except that the secretary shall give notice to the court as soon as reasonably possible after the taking of the person into custody that the person is no longer in treatment pursuant to the Kansas sexually violent predator act and notice to the court when the person is returned to the custody of the secretary for further treatment.

(e) If the court or jury is not satisfied beyond a reasonable doubt that the person is a sexually violent predator, the court shall direct the person's release.

(f) Upon a mistrial, the court shall direct that the person be held at an appropriate secure facility, including, but not limited to, a county jail, until another trial is conducted. Any subsequent trial following a mistrial shall be held within 90 days of the previous trial, unless such subsequent trial is continued as provided in K.S.A. 59-29a06, and amendments thereto.

(g) If the person charged with a sexually violent offense has been found incompetent to stand trial and is about to be released pursuant to K.S.A. 22-3305, and amendments thereto, and such person's commitment is sought pursuant to subsection (a), the court shall first hear evidence and determine whether the person did commit the act or acts charged. The hearing on this issue must comply with all the procedures specified in this section. In addition, the rules of evidence applicable in criminal cases shall apply and all constitutional rights available to defendants at criminal trials, other than the right not to be tried while incompetent, shall apply. After hearing evidence on this issue, the court shall make specific findings on whether the person did commit the act or acts charged, the extent to which the person's incompetence or developmental disability affected the outcome of the hearing, including its effect on the person's ability to consult with and assist counsel and to testify on such person's own behalf, the extent to which the evidence could be reconstructed without the assistance of the person and the strength of the prosecution's case. If after the conclusion of the hearing on this issue, the court finds, beyond a reasonable doubt, that the person did commit the act or acts charged, the court shall enter a final order, appealable by the person, on that issue and may proceed to consider whether the person should be committed pursuant to this section.

K.S.A. 59-29a08. Same; annual examinations; discharge petitions by persons committed under this act over the secretary's objection at time of annual examination, notice to committed person of right, procedure; hearing; transitional release; violating conditions of release.

(a) Each person committed under the Kansas sexually violent predator act shall have a current examination of the person's mental condition made once every year. The secretary shall provide the person with an annual written notice of the person's right to petition the court for release over the secretary's objection. The notice shall contain a waiver of rights. The secretary shall also forward the annual report, as well as the annual notice and waiver form, to the court that committed the person under the Kansas sexually violent predator act. The court shall file the notice and the report upon receipt and forward the file-stamped copy to the attorney general. The attorney general shall forward a file-stamped copy of the annual written notice and annual report to the secretary upon receipt.

(b) The person must file a request for an annual review hearing within 45 days after the date the court files the annual written notice. Failure to request a hearing within 45 days pursuant to this subsection waives the person's right to a hearing until the next annual report is filed by the court. A contested annual review hearing for transitional release shall consist of consideration about whether the person is entitled to transitional release. Only a person in transitional release shall be permitted to petition for conditional release. Only a person in conditional release shall be permitted to petition for final discharge after a minimum of five years has passed in which the person has been free of violations of conditions of such person's treatment plan, as provided in K.S.A. 59-29a19(e), and amendments thereto.

(c) The person may retain, or if the person is indigent and so requests the court may appoint, an examiner pursuant to K.S.A. 60-235, and amendments thereto, and the examiner shall have access to all available records concerning the person. If the person is indigent and makes a request for an examiner, the court shall determine whether the services are necessary and shall determine the reasonable compensation for such services. The court, before appointing an examiner, shall consider factors including the person's compliance with institutional requirements and the person's participation in treatment to determine whether the person's progress justifies the costs of an examination. The appointment of an examiner is discretionary.

(d) At the annual review hearing, the burden of proof shall be upon the person to show probable cause to believe the person's mental abnormality or personality disorder has significantly changed so that the person is safe to be placed in transitional release. The report, or a copy thereof, of the findings of a qualified expert shall be admissible into evidence in the annual review hearing in the same manner and with the same force and effect as if the qualified expert had testified in person. If the person does not participate in the prescribed treatment plan, the person is presumed to be unable to show probable cause to believe the person is safe to be released.

(e) The person shall have a right to have an attorney represent the person at the annual review hearing to determine probable cause, but the person is not entitled to be present at the hearing.

(f) If the person does not file a petition requesting a hearing pursuant to subsection (b), the court that committed the person under the Kansas sexually violent predator act shall then conduct an in camera annual review of the status of the person's mental condition and determine whether the person's mental abnormality or personality disorder has significantly changed so that an annual review hearing is warranted. The court shall enter an order reflecting its determination.

(g) If the court at the annual review hearing determines that probable cause exists to believe that the person's mental abnormality or personality disorder has significantly changed so that the person is safe to be placed in transitional release, then the court shall set a hearing for transitional release on the issue. The person shall be entitled to be present and entitled to the assistance of counsel. The attorney general shall represent the state and shall have a right to have the person evaluated by experts chosen by the state. The person shall also have the right to have experts evaluate the person on the person's behalf and the court shall appoint an expert if the person is indigent and requests an appointment. The burden of proof at the hearing for transitional release shall be upon the state to prove beyond a reasonable doubt that the person's mental abnormality or personality disorder remains such that the person is not safe to be placed in transitional release and if transitionally released is likely to engage in repeat acts of sexual violence.

(h) If, after the hearing for transitional release, the court is convinced beyond a reasonable doubt that the person is not appropriate for transitional release, the court shall order that the person remain in secure commitment. Otherwise, the court shall order that the person be placed in transitional release.

(i) If the court determines that the person should be placed in transitional release, the secretary shall transfer the person to the transitional release program. The secretary may contract for services to be provided in the transitional release program. During any period the person is in transitional release, that person shall comply with any rules or regulations the secretary may establish for this program and every directive of the treatment staff of the transitional release program.

(j) At any time during which the person is in the transitional release program and the treatment staff determines that the person has violated any rule, regulation or directive associated with the transitional release program, the treatment staff may remove the person from the transitional release program and return the person to the secure commitment facility, or may request the district court to issue an emergency ex parte order directing any law enforcement officer to take the person into custody and return the person to the secure commitment facility. Any such request may be made verbally or by telephone, but shall be followed in written, facsimile or electronic form delivered to the court by not later than 5:00 p.m. of the first day the district court is open for the transaction of business after the verbal or telephonic request was made.

(k) Upon the person being returned to the secure commitment facility from the transitional release program, notice thereof shall be given by the secretary to the court. The court shall set the matter for a hearing within two working days of receipt of notice of the person's having been returned to the secure commitment facility and cause notice thereof to be given to the attorney general, the person and the secretary. The attorney general shall have the burden of proof to show probable cause that the person violated conditions of transitional release. The hearing shall be to the court. At the conclusion of the hearing the court shall issue an order returning the person to the secure commitment facility or to the transitional release program, and may order such other further conditions with which the person must comply if the person is returned to the transitional release program.

(l) For the purposes of this section, if the person is indigent and without counsel, the court shall appoint counsel to assist such person.

K.S.A. 59-29a09. Detention and commitment to conform to constitutional requirements.

The involuntary detention or commitment of persons under this act shall conform to constitutional requirements for care and treatment.

K.S.A. 59-29a10. Petition for transitional release; procedure.

(a)

(1) If the secretary determines that the person's mental abnormality

or personality disorder has significantly changed so that the person is not likely to engage in repeat acts of sexual violence if placed in transitional release, the secretary shall authorize the person to petition the court for transitional release. The petition shall be served upon the court and the attorney general. The court, upon service of the petition for transitional release, shall issue notice of a hearing to be scheduled within 30 days. The attorney general shall represent the state, and shall have the right to have the petitioner examined by an expert or professional person of the attorney general's choice. The burden of proof shall be upon the attorney general to show beyond a reasonable doubt that the petitioner's mental abnormality or personality disorder remains such that the petitioner is not safe to be at large and that if placed in transitional release is likely to engage in repeat acts of sexual violence.

(2) If, after the hearing, the court is convinced beyond a reasonable doubt that the person is not sufficiently safe to warrant transitional release, the court shall order that the person remain in secure commitment. Otherwise, the court shall order that the person be placed in transitional release.

(3) The provisions of K.S.A. 59-29a08(i), (j) and (k), and amendments thereto, shall apply to a transitional release pursuant to this section.

(b)

(1) If the secretary determines that the person's mental abnormality or personality disorder has significantly changed so that the person is not likely to engage in repeat acts of sexual violence if placed in conditional release, the secretary shall authorize the person to petition the court for conditional release. The petition shall be served upon the court and the attorney general. The court, upon service of the petition for conditional release, shall issue notice of a hearing to be scheduled within 30 days. The attorney general shall represent the state, and shall have the right to have the petitioner examined by an expert or professional person of the attorney general's choice. The burden of proof shall be upon the attorney general to show beyond a reasonable doubt that the petitioner's mental abnormality or personality disorder remains such that the petitioner is not safe to be at large and that if placed in conditional release is likely to engage in repeat acts of sexual violence.

(2) If, after the hearing, the court is convinced beyond a reasonable doubt that the person is not sufficiently safe to warrant conditional release, the court shall order that the person remain either in secure com-

mitment or in transitional release. Otherwise, the court shall order that the person be placed in conditional release.

(3) The provisions of K.S.A. 59-29a18(h) and 59-29a19(a), (d) and (e), and amendments thereto, shall apply to a conditional release pursuant to this section.

K.S.A. 59-29a11. Transitional release, conditional release or final discharge; subsequent discharge petitions, limitations; prohibition of location of facilities; facilities subject to zoning; county limitations.

(a) If a person has previously filed a petition for transitional release, conditional release or final discharge without the secretary for aging and disability services approval and the court determined either upon review of the petition or following a hearing, that the person's petition was frivolous or that the person's condition had not significantly changed so that it is safe for the person to be at large, then the court shall deny the subsequent petition, unless the petition contains facts upon which a court could find the condition of the petitioner had significantly changed so that a hearing was warranted. Upon receipt of a first or subsequent petition from committed persons without the secretary's approval, the court shall endeavor whenever possible to review the petition and determine if the petition is based upon frivolous grounds and if so shall deny the petition without a hearing.

(b) No transitional release or conditional release facility or building shall be located within 2,000 feet of a licensed child care facility, an established place of worship, any residence in which a child under 18 years of age resides, or the real property of any school upon which is located a structure used by a unified school district or an accredited nonpublic school for student instruction or attendance or extracurricular activities of pupils enrolled in kindergarten or any grades one through 12. This subsection shall not apply to any state institution or facility.

(c) Transitional release or conditional release facilities or buildings shall be subject to all regulations applicable to other property and buildings located in the zone or area that are imposed by any municipality through zoning ordinance, resolution or regulation, such municipality's building regulatory codes, subdivision regulations or other nondiscriminatory regulations.

(d) On and after July 1, 2015, the secretary for aging and disability services shall place no more than 16 sexually violent predators in any one county on transitional release.

(e) The secretary for aging and disability services shall submit an annual report to the governor and the legislature during the first week of the regular legislative session detailing activities related to the transitional release and conditional release of sexually violent predators. The report shall include the status of such predators who have been placed in transitional release or conditional release including the number of any such predators and their locations; information regarding the number of predators who have been returned to the sexually violent predator treatment program at Larned state hospital along with the reasons for such return; and any plans for the development of additional transitional release or conditional release facilities.

K.S.A. 59-29a12. Same; secretary of social and rehabilitation services; responsible for costs; duties; reimbursement; costs paid by committed person.

(a) For state budgetary purposes, the secretary shall be responsible for all cost relating to the evaluation and treatment of persons committed to the secretary's custody under any provision of this act. Payment for the maintenance, care and treatment of any such committed person shall be paid by the person, by the conservator of such person's estate or by any person bound by law to support such person. Reimbursement may be obtained by the secretary for the cost of care and treatment, including placement in transitional release, of persons committed to the secretary's custody pursuant to K.S.A. 59-2006, and amendments thereto.

(b) When a court orders a person committed to the secretary's custody under any provision of this act to appear at a court proceeding, the county where such court is located shall be responsible for the transportation, security and control of such person and all costs involved. The secretary shall not be required to provide an employee to travel with the committed person.

(c) Except as provided further, when a court proceeding is initiated by the committed person, such person shall be responsible for making all arrangements concerning the transportation, security and control of such person and all costs involved. The secretary shall review and approve all arrangements prior to the court proceeding. The secretary may deny the arrangements if such arrangements fail to meet security standards. The provisions of this subsection shall not apply to a hearing pursuant to

K.S.A. 59-29a08, and amendments thereto.

(d) The secretary shall adopt rules and regulations to implement this section.

K.S.A. 59-29a13. Same; notice to victims of release of persons committed under this act.

In addition to any other information required to be released under this act, prior to the release of a person committed under this act, the secretary shall give written notice of such placement or release to any victim of the person's activities or crime who is alive and whose address is known to the secretary.

Failure to notify shall not be a reason for postponement of release. Nothing in this section shall create a cause of action against the state or an employee of the state acting within the scope of the employee's employment as a result of the failure to notify pursuant to this action.

K.S.A. 59-29a14. Same; special allegation of sexual motivation; procedure; withdrawal or dismissal.

(a) The county or district attorney shall file a special allegation of sexual motivation within 14 days after arraignment in every criminal case other than sex offenses as defined in article 35 of chapter 21 of the Kansas Statutes Annotated, prior to their repeal, or article 55 of chapter 21 of the Kansas Statutes Annotated, or K.S.A. 2014 Supp. 21-6419 through 21-6422, and amendments thereto, when sufficient admissible evidence exists, which, when considered with the most plausible, reasonably foreseeable defense that could be raised under the evidence, would justify a finding of sexual motivation by a reasonable and objective fact finder.

(b) In a criminal case wherein there has been a special allegation, the state shall prove beyond a reasonable doubt that the accused committed the crime with a sexual motivation. The court shall make a finding of fact of whether or not a sexual motivation was present at the time of the commission of the crime, or if a jury trial is had, the jury, if it finds the defendant guilty, also shall find a special verdict as to whether or not the defendant committed the crime with a sexual motivation. This finding shall not be applied to sex offenses as defined in article 35 of chapter 21 of the Kansas Statutes Annotated, prior to their repeal, or article 55 of chapter 21 of the Kansas Statutes Annotated, or K.S.A. 2014 Supp. 21-

6419 through 21-6422, and amendments thereto.

(c) The county or district attorney shall not withdraw the special alle-gation of sexual motivation without approval of the court through an or-der of dismissal of the special allegation. The court shall not dismiss this special allegation unless it finds that such an order is necessary to correct an error in the initial charging decision or unless there are evidentiary problems which make proving the special allegation doubtful.

K.S.A. 59-29a15. Same; severability.

If any provision of this act or the application thereof to any person or circumstances is held invalid, the invalidity shall not affect other pro-visions or applications of the act which can be given effect without the invalid provisions or application and, to this end, the provisions of this act are severable.

K.S.A. 59-29a16. Same; confidential or privileged information and re-cords.

In order to protect the public, relevant information and records which are otherwise confidential or privileged shall be released to the agency with jurisdiction or the attorney general for the purpose of meeting the notice requirement provided in K.S.A. 59-29a03 and amendments there-to and determining whether a person is or continues to be a sexually violent predator. The provisions of this section shall be part of and sup-plemental to the provisions of K.S.A. 59-29a01 through 59-29a15 and amendments thereto.

K.S.A. 59-29a17. Same; court records; sealed and opened by court order.

Any psychological reports, drug and alcohol reports, treatment re-cords, reports of the diagnostic center, medical records or victim impact statements which have been submitted to the court or admitted into ev-idence under this act shall be part of the record but shall be sealed and opened only on order of the court or as provided in K.S.A. 59-29a01 et seq. and amendments thereto. The provisions of this section shall be part of and supplemental to the provisions of K.S.A. 59-29a01 through 59-29a15 and amendments thereto.

K.S.A. 59-29a18. Conditional release; examination by staff; report; review and hearing by court; orders.

(a) During any period the person is in transitional release, the person committed under this act at least annually, and at any other time deemed appropriate by the treatment staff, shall be examined by the treatment staff to determine if the person's mental abnormality or personality disorder has significantly changed so as to warrant such person being considered for conditional release. The secretary shall provide the person with a written notice of the person's right to petition the court for release over the secretary's objection. The notice shall contain a waiver of rights. The secretary shall also forward the report, as well as the notice and waiver form, to the court that committed the person under the Kansas sexually violent predator act. The court shall file the notice and the report upon receipt.

(b) The person must file a request for an annual review hearing within 45 days after the date the court files the annual written notice pursuant to subsection (a). Failure to request a hearing within 45 days pursuant to this subsection shall waive the person's right to a hearing until the next annual report is filed by the court. A contested annual review hearing for conditional release shall consist of consideration about whether the person is entitled to conditional release from transitional release. Only a person in transitional release shall be permitted to petition for conditional release. No person in transitional release shall be permitted to petition for final discharge.

(c) The person may retain, or if the person is indigent and so requests, the court may appoint, an examiner pursuant to K.S.A. 60-235, and amendments thereto, and the examiner shall have access to all available records concerning the person. If the person is indigent and makes a request for an examiner, the court shall determine whether the services are necessary and shall determine the reasonable compensation for such services. The court, before appointing an examiner, shall consider factors including the person's compliance with institutional requirements and the person's participation in treatment to determine whether the person's progress justifies the costs of an examination. The appointment of an examiner is discretionary.

(d) At the annual review hearing, the burden of proof shall be upon the person to show probable cause to believe the person's mental abnormality or personality disorder has significantly changed so that the person is safe to be placed in conditional release. The report, or a copy thereof, of the findings of a qualified expert shall be admissible into evidence in the annual review hearing in the same manner and with the same force and effect as if the qualified expert had testified in person. If the person does not participate in the prescribed treatment plan, the person is presumed to be unable to show probable cause to believe the person is safe to be released.

(e) The person shall have a right to have an attorney represent the person at the annual review hearing to determine probable cause, but the person is not entitled to be present at the hearing.

(f) If the person does not file a petition requesting a hearing pursuant to subsection (b), the court that committed the person under the Kansas sexually violent predator act shall then conduct an in camera annual review of the status of the person's mental condition and determine whether the person's mental abnormality or personality disorder has significantly changed so that an annual review hearing is warranted. The court shall enter an order reflecting its determination.

(g) If the court at the annual review hearing determines that probable cause exists to believe that the person's mental abnormality or personality disorder has significantly changed so that the person is safe to be placed in conditional release, then the court shall set a hearing for conditional release on the issue. The person shall be entitled to be present and entitled to the assistance of counsel. The attorney general shall represent the state and shall have a right to have the person evaluated by experts chosen by the state. The person shall also have the right to have experts evaluate the person on the person's behalf and the court shall appoint an expert if the person is indigent and requests an appointment. The burden of proof at the hearing for conditional release shall be upon the state to prove beyond a reasonable doubt that the person's mental abnormality or personality disorder remains such that the person is not safe to be placed in conditional release and if conditionally released is likely to engage in repeat acts of sexual violence.

(h) If, after the hearing for conditional release, the court is convinced beyond a reasonable doubt that the person is not appropriate for conditional release, the court shall order that the person remain either in secure commitment or in transitional release. Otherwise, the court shall order that the person be placed on conditional release.

(i) Subsequent to either a court review or a hearing, the court shall issue an appropriate order with findings of fact. The order of the court shall be provided to the attorney general, the person and the secretary.

(j) For the purposes of this section, if the person is indigent and without counsel, the court shall appoint counsel to assist such person.

K.S.A. 59-29a19. Conditional release; plan of treatment; minimum term; hearing for final release; violating conditions of plan or release.

(a) If the court determines that the person should be placed on conditional release, the court, based upon the recommendation of the treatment staff and progress review panel, shall establish a plan of treatment which the person shall be ordered to follow. This plan of treatment may include, but shall not be limited to: Provisions as to where the person shall reside and with whom, taking prescribed medications, attending individual and group counseling and any other type of treatment, maintaining employment, having no contact with children, having no direct contact with individuals that match the person's victim template, travel restrictions, searches, home visits, substance abuse testing and registration requirements. Upon a showing by the person that the person accepts the plan of treatment and is prepared to follow it, the court shall release the person from the transitional release program.

(b) The conditional release monitor shall monitor the person's compliance with the plan of treatment ordered by the court while on conditional release. The conditional release monitor shall report the person's progress on conditional release to the court. At any time during which the person is on conditional release and the conditional release monitor determines that the person has violated any material condition of the plan, the conditional release monitor may request the district court to issue an emergency ex parte order directing any law enforcement officer to take the person into custody and return the person to the secure commitment facility. Any such request shall be made by sworn affidavit setting forth with specificity the grounds for the entry of such emergency ex parte order provided to the court by personal deliver, telefacsimile communication or electronic means prior to the entry of such order and notice of such request shall be given to the person's counsel, or if the person is unrepresented, to the person.

(c) A current examination of the person's mental condition shall be made in accordance with K.S.A. 59-29a08, and amendments thereto, and submitted to the court and the secretary once each year.

(d) Upon the person being returned to the secure commitment facility from conditional release, notice shall be given by the secretary to the court. The court shall set the matter for a hearing within two working days of receipt of notice of the person's having been returned to the secure commitment facility and cause notice to be given to the attorney general, the person and the secretary. The attorney general shall have the burden of proof to show probable cause that the person violated conditions of conditional release. The hearing shall be to the court. At the conclusion of the hearing, the court shall issue an order returning the person to the secure commitment facility, to transitional release, or to conditional release, and may order such other further conditions with which the person must comply if the person is returned to either transitional release or conditional release.

(e) After a minimum of five years has passed in which the person has been free of violations of conditions of such person's treatment plan, the treatment staff, or other treatment providers directed by the court, may examine such person to determine if the person's mental abnormality or personality disorder has significantly changed so as to warrant such person being considered for final discharge. The individual preparing the report shall forward the report to the court. The court shall review the same. If the court determines that probable cause exists to believe that the person's mental abnormality or personality disorder has so changed that the person is safe to be entitled to final discharge, the court shall set a formal hearing on the issue. The attorney general shall have the burden of proof to show beyond a reasonable doubt that the person's mental abnormality or personality disorder remains such that such person is not appropriate for final discharge. The person shall have the same rights as enumerated in K.S.A. 59-29a06, and amendments thereto. Subsequent to either a court review or a hearing, the court shall issue an appropriate order with findings of fact. The order of the court shall be provided to the attorney general, the person and the secretary.

(f) If, after a hearing, the court is convinced beyond a reasonable doubt that the person is not appropriate for final discharge, the court shall continue custody of the person with the secretary for placement in a secure facility, or on transitional or conditional release. Otherwise, the court shall order the person finally discharged. In the event the court does not order final discharge of the person, the person still retains the right to annual reviews.

(g) The final discharge shall not prevent the person from being prosecuted for any criminal acts which the person is alleged to have committed or from being subject in the future to a subsequent commitment under this act.

K.S.A. 59-29a20. Bail, bond, house arrest or other release; not eligible.

Any person for whom a petition pursuant to this act has been filed and is in the secure confinement of the state shall not be eligible for bail, bond, house arrest or any other measures releasing the person from the physical protective custody of the state, notwithstanding the provisions of K.S.A. 59-29a10 and amendments thereto.

K.S.A. 59-29a21. Severability.

If any provision of this act * or the application thereof to any person or circumstances is held invalid, the invalidity shall not affect other provisions or applications of the act which can be given effect without the invalid provisions or application and, to this end, the provisions of this act are severable.

K.S.A. 59-29a22. Sexually violent predators; rights and rules of conduct; definitions.

(a) As used in this section:

(1) "Person" means any individual:

(A) Who is receiving services for mental illness and who is admitted, detained, committed, transferred or placed in the custody of the secretary for aging and disability services under the authority of K.S.A. 22-3219, 22-3302, 22-3303, 22-3428a, 22-3429, 22-3430, 59-29a05, 75-5209 and 76-1306, and amendments thereto.

(B) In the custody of the secretary for aging and disability services after being found a sexually violent predator pursuant to the Kansas sexually violent predator act, including any sexually violent predator placed on transitional release.

(2) "Restraints" means the application of any devices, other than human force alone, to any part of the body of the person for the purpose of preventing the person from causing injury to self or others.

(3) "Seclusion" means the placement of a person, alone, in a room, where the person's freedom to leave is restricted and where the person is not under continuous observation.

(4) "Emergency lockdown" means a safety measure used to isolate all

or a designated number of persons greater than one to their rooms for a period necessary to ensure a safe and secure environment.

(5) "Individual person management plan" means a safety measure used to isolate an individual person when the person presents a safety or security risk that cannot be addressed through routine psychiatric methods.

(b) Each person shall have the following statutory rights:

(1) Upon admission or commitment, to be informed orally and in writing of the person's rights under this section. Copies of this section shall be posted conspicuously in each facility, and shall be available to the person's guardian and immediate family.

(2) To refuse to perform labor which is of financial benefit to the facility in which the person is receiving treatment or service. Privileges or release from the facility may not be conditioned upon the performance of any labor which is regulated by this subsection. Tasks of a personal housekeeping nature are not considered compensable labor. A person may voluntarily engage in therapeutic labor which is of financial benefit to the facility if such labor is compensated in accordance with a plan approved by the department and if:

(A) The labor is an integrated part of the person's treatment plan;

(B) The labor is supervised by a staff member who is qualified to oversee the therapeutic aspects of the activity;

(C) The person has given written informed consent to engage in such labor and has been informed that such consent may be withdrawn at any time; and

(D) The labor involved is evaluated for its appropriateness by the staff of the facility at least once every 180 days.

(3) To receive adequate treatment appropriate for such person's condition.

(4) To be informed of such person's treatment and care and to participate in the planning of such treatment and care.

(5) To refuse to consent to the administration of any medication prescribed for medical or psychiatric treatment, except in a situation in which the person is in a mental health crisis and less restrictive or intrusive measures have proven to be inadequate or clinically inappropriate. Treatment for a mental health crisis shall include medication or treatment necessary to prevent serious physical harm to the person or to others. After full explanation of the benefits and risks of such medication, the

medication may be administered over the person's objection, except that the objection shall be recorded in the person's medical record and at the same time written notice thereof shall be forwarded to the medical director of the treatment facility or the director's designee. Within five days after receiving such notice, excluding Saturdays, Sundays and legal holidays, the medical director or designee shall deliver to the person's medical provider the medical director's or designee's written decision concerning the administration of that medication, and a copy of that decision shall be placed in the person's medical record.

(A) Medication may not be used as punishment, for the convenience of staff, as a substitute for a treatment program or in quantities that interfere with a person's treatment program.

(B) A person will have the right to have explained the nature of all medications prescribed, the reason for the prescription and the most common side effects and, if requested, the nature of any other treatments ordered.

(6) To be subjected to restraint, seclusion, emergency lockdown, individual person management plan, or any combination thereof, only as provided in this subsection.

(A) Restraints, seclusion, or both, may be used in the following circumstances:

(i) If it is determined by medical staff to be necessary to prevent immediate substantial bodily injury to the person or others and that other alternative methods to prevent such injury are not sufficient to accomplish this purpose. When used, the extent of the restraint or seclusion applied to the person shall be the least restrictive measure necessary to prevent such injury to the person or others, and the use of restraint or seclusion in a treatment facility shall not exceed three hours without medical reevaluation. When restraints or seclusion are applied, there shall be monitoring of the person's condition at a frequency determined by the treating physician or licensed psychologist, which shall be no less than once per each 30 minutes. The superintendent of the treatment facility or a physician or licensed psychologist shall sign a statement explaining the treatment necessity for the use of any restraint or seclusion and shall make such statement a part of the permanent treatment record of the person.

(ii) For security reasons during transport to or from the person's unit, including, but not limited to, transport to another treatment or health care facility, another secure facility or court. Any person committed or transferred to a hospital or other health care facility for medical care may be isolated for security reasons within a locked area.

(B) Emergency lockdown may be used in the following circumstances:

(i) When necessary as an emergency measure as needed for security purposes, to deal with an escape or attempted escape, the discovery of a dangerous weapon or explosive device in the unit or facility or the receipt of reliable information that a dangerous weapon or explosive device is in the unit or facility, to prevent or control a riot or the taking of a hostage or for the discovery of contraband or a unit-wide search. An emergency lockdown order may be authorized only by the superintendent of the facility or the superintendent's designee.

(ii) During a period of emergency lockdown, the status of each person shall be reviewed every 30 minutes to ensure the safety of the person, and each person who is locked in a room without a toilet shall be given an opportunity to use a toilet at least once every hour, or more frequently if medically indicated.

(iii) The facility shall have a written policy covering the use of emergency lockdown that ensures the safety of the individual is secured and that there is regular, frequent monitoring by trained staff to care for bodily needs as may be required.

(iv) An emergency lockdown order may only be in effect for the period of time needed to preserve order while dealing with the situation and may not be used as a substitute for adequate staffing.

(C) Individual person management plan may be used in any of the following situations:

(i) As needed when a person demonstrates or threatens substantial injury to others, and routine psychiatric methods have been ineffective or are unlikely to be effective in reducing such risk.

(ii) As needed for safety or security purposes, for the behavioral management in situations including, but not limited to:

(a) Dealing with an escape or attempted escape;

(b) The discovery of a dangerous weapon or explosive device in the unit or facility or the receipt of reliable information that a dangerous weapon or explosive device is in the unit or facility;

(c) Preventing or controlling a riot;

(d) The taking of a hostage;

(e) The disruption of the therapeutic environment on the unit; or

(f) For the discovery of contraband.

(iii) The status of the person shall be reviewed every 30 minutes to ensure the safety of the person.

(D) Restraint, seclusion, emergency lockdown, individual person management plan, or any combination thereof, may be used in any other situation deemed necessary by treatment staff for the safety of a person or persons, facility staff or visitors. In all situations, restraint, seclusion, emergency lockdown, or individual person management plan shall never be used as a punishment or for the convenience of staff.

(E) A person may be locked or restricted in such person's room during the night shift if such person resides in a unit in which each room is equipped with a toilet and sink or, if a person does not have a toilet in the room, if such person is given an opportunity to use a toilet at least once every hour, or more frequently if medically indicated.

(7) To not be subject to such procedures as psychosurgery, electro-shock therapy, experimental medication, aversion therapy or hazardous treatment procedures without the written consent of the person or the written consent of a parent or legal guardian, if such person is a minor or has a legal guardian provided that the guardian has obtained authority to consent to such from the court which has venue over the guardianship following a hearing held for that purpose.

(8) To individual religious worship within the facility if the person desires such an opportunity, as long as it complies with applicable laws and facility rules and policies. The provisions for worship shall be available to all persons on a nondiscriminatory basis. No individual may be coerced into engaging in any religious activities.

(9) To a humane psychological and physical environment within the hospital facilities. All facilities shall be designed to afford patients with comfort and safety, to promote dignity and ensure privacy. Facilities shall also be designed to make a positive contribution to the effective attainment of the treatment goals of the hospital.

(10) To confidentiality of all treatment records and, as permitted by other applicable state or federal laws, to inspect and, upon receipt of payment of reasonable costs, to receive a copy of such records. The head of any treatment facility or designee who has the records may refuse to disclose portions of such records if the head of the treatment facility or designee states in writing that such disclosure will likely be injurious to the welfare of the person.

(11) Except as otherwise provided, to not be filmed or taped, unless the person signs an informed and voluntary consent that specifically authorizes a named individual or group to film or tape the person for a particular purpose or project during a specified time period. The person may specify in such consent periods during which, or situations in which, the person may not be filmed or taped. If a person is legally incompetent, such consent shall be granted on behalf of the person by the person's guardian. A person may be filmed or taped for security purposes without the person's consent.

(12) To be informed in writing upon or at a reasonable time after admission, of any liability that the patient or any of the patient's relatives may have for the cost of the patient's care and treatment and of the right to receive information about charges for care and treatment services.

(13) To be treated with respect and recognition of the patient's dignity and individuality by all employees of the treatment facility.

(14) To send and receive sealed mail to or from legal counsel, the courts, the secretary for aging and disability services, the superintendent of the treatment facility, the agency designated as the developmental disabilities protection and advocacy agency pursuant to P.L. 94-103, as amended, private physicians and licensed psychologists. A person who is indigent may have reasonable access to letter-writing materials.

(15) To send and receive mail with reasonable limitations. A person's mail is subject to physical examination and inspection for contraband, as defined by facility rules and policies.

(A) An officer or employee of the facility at which the person is placed may delay delivery of the mail to the person for a reasonable period of time to verify whether the mail contains contraband, as defined by facility rules and policies, or whether the person named as the sender actually sent the mail. If contraband is found, such contraband may be returned to the sender or confiscated by the facility. If the officer or staff member cannot determine whether the person named as the sender actually sent the mail, the officer or staff member may return the mail to the sender along with notice of the facility mail policy.

(B) The superintendent of the facility or the superintendent's designee may, in accordance with the standards and the procedure under subsection (c), authorize a member of the facility treatment staff to read the mail, if the superintendent or the superintendent's designee has reason to believe that the mail could pose a threat to security at the facility or seriously interfere with the treatment, rights, or safety of the person or others.

(C) A person may not receive through the mail any sexually explicit materials, items that are considered contraband, as defined by facility rules and policies, or items deemed to jeopardize the person's individual treatment, another person's treatment or the therapeutic environment of the facility.

(16) Reasonable access to a telephone to make and receive telephone calls within reasonable limits.

(17) To wear and use such person's own clothing and toilet articles, as long as such wear and use complies with facility rules and policies, or to be furnished with an adequate allowance of clothes if none are available.

(18) To possess personal property in a reasonable amount, as long as the property complies with state laws and facility rules and policies, and be provided a reasonable amount of individual storage space pursuant to facility rules and policies. In no event shall a person be allowed to possess or store contraband.

(19) Reasonable protection of privacy in such matters as toileting and bathing.

(20) To see a reasonable number of visitors who do not pose a threat to the safety and security or therapeutic climate of the person, other persons, visitors or the facility.

(21) To present grievances under the procedures established by each facility on the person's own behalf.

(22) To spend such person's money as such person chooses with reasonable limitations, except under the following circumstances: (A) When restricted by facility rules and policies; or (B) to the extent that authority over the money is held by another, including the parent of a minor, a court-appointed guardian of the person's estate or a representative payee. A treatment facility may, as a part of its security procedures, use a trust account in lieu of currency that is held by a person, and may establish reasonable policies governing account transactions.

(c)

(1) A person's rights under subsections (b)(15) to (b)(22) may be denied for cause by the superintendent of the facility or the superintendent's designee, or when medically or therapeutically contraindicated as documented by the person's physician, licensed psychologist or licensed master's level psychologist in the person's treatment record. The individ-

ual shall be informed in writing of the grounds for withdrawal of the right and shall have the opportunity for a review of the withdrawal of the right in an informal hearing before the superintendent of the facility or the superintendent's designee. There shall be documentation of the grounds for withdrawal of rights in the person's treatment record.

(2) Notwithstanding subsection (c)(1), when the facility makes an administrative decision that applies equally to all persons and there is a legitimate governmental reason for the decision, notice of the decision is all that is required.

(d) The secretary for aging and disability services shall establish procedures to assure protection of persons' rights guaranteed under this section.

(e) No person may intentionally retaliate or discriminate against any person or employee for contacting or providing information to any state official or to an employee of any state protection and advocacy agency, or for initiating, participating in, or testifying in a grievance procedure or in an action for any remedy authorized under this section.

(f)

(1) Proceedings under this section or any other appeal concerning an action by the Kansas department for aging and disability services shall be governed under the Kansas administrative procedure act and the Kansas judicial review act. A person appealing any alleged violations of this section or any other agency determination shall exhaust all administrative remedies available through the Larned state hospital, including the sexual predator treatment program, before having any right to request a hearing under the Kansas administrative procedure act.

(2) A final agency determination shall include notice of the right to appeal such determination only to the office of administrative hearings. Within 30 days after service of a final agency determination and the notice of right to appeal, the appellant may file a request for hearing in writing with the office of administrative hearings for a review of that determination. Any request for hearing must be accompanied by a copy of the final agency determination, including all documentation submitted through Larned state hospital and all agency responses. Failure to timely request a hearing constitutes a waiver of the right to any review. The request shall be examined by the presiding officer assigned. If the appellant seeks to challenge the final agency determination on any grounds other than material facts in controversy or agency violation of a relevant rule,

regulation or statute, the appellant shall express such allegations with particularity within the request for hearing. If it plainly appears from the face of the request and accompanying final agency determination that the appellant failed to state a claim on which relief could be granted, or the appellant failed to demonstrate exhaustion, the request shall be dismissed. The burden shall be on the appellant to prove by a preponderance of the evidence that the agency action violated a specific rule, regulation or statute. If the request for hearing does not allege a violation of a specific rule, regulation or statute, the burden shall be on the appellant to prove by a preponderance of the evidence that the agency had no legitimate government interest in taking such action. Any dispositive ruling of the hearing officer assigned by the office of administrative hearings shall be deemed an initial order under the Kansas administrative procedure act.

(3) The person shall participate by telephone or other electronic means at any hearing before the office of administrative hearings or any proceeding under the Kansas judicial review act, unless the presiding officer or court determines that the interests of justice require an in-person proceeding. Notwithstanding K.S.A. 77-609, and amendments thereto, if an in-person proceeding is necessary, such proceeding shall be conducted at the place where the person is committed.

(4) Except as otherwise provided in the Kansas sexually violent predator act and notwithstanding K.S.A. 77-609, and amendments thereto, venue shall be in Pawnee county, Kansas, for all proceedings brought pursuant to the Kansas judicial review act.

K.S.A. 59-29a23. Habeas corpus petition; costs related thereto.

(a) Whenever a person civilly committed pursuant to the Kansas sexually violent predator act files any civil action relating to such commitment, including, but not limited to, an action pursuant to K.S.A. 60-1501 et seq., and amendments thereto, the costs incurred, including, but not limited to, the filing fee, costs of appointed counsel fees and expenses, witness fees and expenses, expert fees and expenses and other expenses related to the prosecution and defense of such petition, shall be taxed to the civilly committed person bringing the action.

(b)

(1) Subject to subsection (c), any court may authorize the commencement of any civil action, or appeal therein, without prepayment of fees

or security therefore, by a civilly committed person who submits an affidavit that includes a statement of all assets that such person possesses and a statement that such person is unable to pay such fees or give security therefore. Such affidavit shall state the nature of the civil action or appeal and the affiant's belief that the person is entitled to redress.

(2) A civilly committed person seeking to bring a civil action, or appeal therein, without prepayment of fees or security therefore, in addition to filing the affidavit required by subsection (b)(1), shall submit a certified copy of the trust fund account statement, or institutional equivalent, for such person for the six-month period immediately preceding the filing of the action or notice of appeal, obtained from the appropriate official of each facility at which such person is or was committed. In addition, such person shall submit a certified copy of all private banking account and investment account statements for the six-month period immediately preceding the filing of the action or notice of appeal for which the person is the account owner or beneficiary.

(3) If the court determines, based on the affidavit and information provided pursuant to this subsection, that the person is indigent, the costs incurred shall be taxed to the county responsible for the costs.

(4) Any district court receiving a statement of costs from another district court shall forthwith approve the same for payment out of the general fund of its county, except that it may refuse to approve the same for payment only on the ground that it is not the county responsible for the costs. If the claim for costs is not paid within 120 days, an action may be maintained thereon by the claimant county in the district court of the claimant county against the debtor county.

(5) The county responsible for the costs incurred pursuant to this subsection shall be reimbursed for such costs by the office of the attorney general from the sexually violent predator expense fund. The attorney general shall develop and implement a procedure to provide such reimbursements. If there are no moneys available in such fund to pay any such reimbursements, the county may file a claim against the state pursuant to article 9 of chapter 46, of the Kansas Statutes Annotated, and amendments thereto.

(6) An appeal may not be taken in forma pauperis if the trial court certifies in writing that such appeal is not taken in good faith.

(c)

(1) Notwithstanding subsection (b), if a civilly committed person

brings a civil action or files an appeal in forma pauperis, such person shall be required to pay the full amount of a filing fee. The court shall assess and, when funds exist, collect as a partial payment of any court fees required by law, an initial partial filing fee of 20% of the greater of:

(A) The average monthly deposits to the civilly committed person's trust account, or institutional equivalent; or

(B) The average monthly balance in the civilly committed person's trust account, or institutional equivalent, for the six-month period immediately preceding the filing of the action or notice of appeal.

(2) After payment of the initial partial filing fee, the civilly committed person shall be required to make monthly payments of 20% of the preceding month's income credited to the civilly committed person's account. The agency having custody of the civilly committed person shall forward payments from the civilly committed person's account to the clerk of the court each time the amount in the account exceeds $10 until the filing fees are paid. The clerk shall then forward the payments to the county responsible for the costs for reimbursement.

(3) In no event shall the filing fee collected exceed the amount of fees permitted by statute for the commencement of a civil action or an appeal of a civil action.

(4) In no event shall a civilly committed person be prohibited from bringing a civil action or appealing a civil action for the reason that such person has no assets and no means by which to pay the initial partial filing fee.

(d) Notwithstanding any filing fee, or any portion thereof, that may have been paid, the court shall dismiss the case at any time if the court determines that:

(1) The allegation of poverty is untrue; or

(2) The action or appeal:

(A) Is frivolous or malicious;

(B) Fails to state a claim on which relief may be granted; or

(C) Seeks monetary relief against a defendant who is immune from such relief.

(e)

(1) Judgment may be rendered for costs at the conclusion of the suit or action as in other proceedings.

(2)

(A) If the judgment against a civilly committed person includes the payment of costs under this subsection, such person shall be required to pay the full amount of the costs ordered.

(B) The civilly committed person shall be required to make payments for costs under this subsection in the same manner provided for filing fees under subsection (c).

(C) In no event shall the costs collected exceed the amount of the costs ordered by the court.

(f) In no event shall a civilly committed person bring a civil action or appeal a judgment in a civil action or proceeding in forma pauperis if such person has, on three or more prior occasions, while confined in any facility, brought an action or appeal in a court of the state of Kansas or of the United States that was dismissed on the grounds that it was frivolous, malicious or failed to state a claim upon which relief may be granted, unless such person is under imminent danger of serious physical injury.

(g) As used in this section, "county responsible for the costs" means the county where the person was determined to be a sexually violent predator pursuant to the Kansas Sexually Violent Predator Act.

K.S.A. 59-29a24. Civil actions; exhaustion of administrative remedies required.

Any person civilly committed pursuant to the Kansas sexually violent predator act, prior to filing any civil action, including, but not limited to, an action pursuant to K.S.A. 60-1501 et seq., and amendments thereto, naming as the defendant the state of Kansas, any political subdivision of the state of Kansas, any public official, the secretary for aging and disability services or an employee of the Kansas department for aging and disability services, while such employee is engaged in the performance of such employee's duty, shall be required to have exhausted all administrative remedies concerning such civil action. Upon filing a petition in a civil action, such person shall file with such petition proof that all administrative remedies have been exhausted.

K.S.A. 59-29a25 Effect of permanent physiological change on commitment.

(a) Whenever there is current evidence since the last annual examination from an expert or professional person that an identified physiological change to the committed person, such as paralysis, stroke or dementia, renders the committed person unable to commit a sexually violent offense and that this change is permanent, the person may petition the court for a hearing to be released.

(b) If the court finds after a hearing that the person has demonstrated by clear and convincing evidence that the person suffers from a permanent physiological change rendering the person unable to commit a sexually violent offense, the court shall discharge the person from the program and notify the secretary. At the hearing, the person shall have the right to counsel. The state shall have the right to have the person examined before the hearing. The burden of proof shall be on the person to prove the physiological change is permanent and renders the person unable to commit a sexually violent offense.

(c) If the court finds the person has not suffered a permanent physiological change or is not safe, the person shall remain in secure commitment.

(d) This section shall be a part of and supplemental to the Kansas Sexually Violent Predator Act.

K.S.A. 59-29a26 County responsible for costs.

(a) The cost of any post-commitment hearings, annual review hearings, including those provided by the office of administrative hearings, evaluations or other expenses expressly provided for in the Kansas sexually violent predator act shall be paid by the county responsible for the costs.

(b) The cost of any sexual predator treatment program administrative hearings involving K.S.A. 2014 Supp. 59-29a22, and amendments thereto, or other program decisions appealed to or received by the office of administrative hearings shall be paid by the county responsible for the costs.

(c) At the conclusion of any of the proceedings described in this section, the office of administrative hearings shall provide a statement to the county responsible for the costs. The county shall pay the office of administrative hearings within 60 days following the receipt of the bill or prior to the expiration of the fiscal year in which the costs were incurred, whichever occurs first.

(d) As used in this section, "county responsible for the costs" means the county where the person was determined to be a sexually violent predator pursuant to the Kansas sexually violent predator act.

(e) This section shall be a part of and supplemental to the Kansas Sexually Violent Predator Act.

K.S.A. 59-29a27 Duty of care pending criminal proceedings; Reimbursement of costs.

(a)

(1) Whenever a person civilly committed pursuant to K.S.A. 59-29a07, and amendments thereto, is in the custody of a county law enforcement agency for a pending criminal proceeding, the costs incurred for the care and custody of such person by the county with custody of such person, including, but not limited to, reasonable costs of medical care and treatment, housing, food and transportation, shall be paid by such county.

(2) The secretary for aging and disability services shall reimburse such county from the Larned state hospital — SPTP new crimes reimbursement account of the state general fund for all costs that would have been paid from such account if such person had remained in the custody of the secretary for aging and disability services.

(b)

(1) Whenever a person civilly committed pursuant to K.S.A. 59-29a07, and amendments thereto, commits a crime and is prosecuted for such crime, the costs incurred for such prosecution shall be paid by the county where such prosecution occurs.

(2) The secretary for aging and disability services shall reimburse such county from the Larned state hospital — SPTP new crimes reimbursement account of the state general fund for all reasonable costs incurred for such prosecution.

(c) If there are no moneys available in the Larned state hospital — SPTP new crimes reimbursement account of the state general fund to pay any reimbursements described in subsection (a) or (b), the county entitled to such reimbursement may file a claim against the state pursuant to article 9 of chapter 46 of the Kansas Statutes Annotated, and amendments thereto.

(d) The secretary for aging and disability services shall develop and implement a procedure to provide the reimbursements described in subsections (a) and (b) on or before January 1, 2016.

(e) All expenditures pursuant to this section from the Larned state hospital — SPTP new crimes reimbursement account of the state general fund shall be made in accordance with appropriation acts upon warrants of the director of accounts and reports issued pursuant to vouchers approved by the secretary for aging and disability services or the secretary's designee.

Chapter 5

Ancillary Statutes to the KSVPA

The KSVPA is not a stand-alone statutory act. It is supported by other laws in Kansas and some of these other laws put rules and duties upon the person committed under the KSVPA. There is a criminal statute to define contraband and the penalty for contraband while committed under the KSVPA. Then there is the Kansas Registration Offender Act (KORA) that was made applicable to all committed persons under the KSVPA. The final statute is a criminal statute defining what battery on a mental health employee is and the consequences for said offense.

These three statutes were not in effect when the KSVPA was enacted. Rather at the request of the agency confining individuals under the KSVPA or the public the Legislature created these laws to put more restrictions upon one labeled as a Sexually Violent Predator. It is true that for most under the KSVPA these statutes enhanced their criminal sentence, but the Courts hold them to not be ex post facto laws or punitive laws and therefore constitutionally valid.

I. Contraband

In the year 2009 the Kansas Legislature Amended the Traffic in Contraband statute through Senate Bill 237. This amendment was to make it a felony for a person confined under the KSVPA to have or traffic contraband within the facility. After the KSVPA had been in practice for fifteen years the State deemed it necessary to set that contraband within the care and treatment facility under the KSVPA is a felony. One may question why did it take so long?

The State of Kansas revamped the Criminal Code and the Contraband Statute, which was K.S.A. § 21-3826, became the statute now cited as K.S.A. § 21-5914. The statute reads as follows:

21-5914. Traffic in contraband in a correctional institution or care and treatment facility.

(a) Traffic in contraband in a correctional institution or care and treatment facility is, without the consent of the administrator of the correctional institution or care and treatment facility:

(1) Introducing or attempting to introduce any item into or upon the grounds of any correctional institution or care and treatment facility;

(2) Taking, sending, attempting to take or attempting to send any item from any correctional institution or care and treatment facility;

(3) Any unauthorized possession of any item while in any correctional institution or care and treatment facility;

(4) Distributing any item within any correctional institution or care and treatment facility;

(5) Supplying to another who is in lawful custody any object or thing adapted or designed for use in making an escape; or

(6) Introducing into an institution in which a person is confined any object or thing adapted or designed for use in making any escape.

(b) Traffic in contraband in a correctional institution or care and treatment facility is a:

(1) Severity level 6, nonperson felony, except as provided in subsection (b)(2) or (b)(3);

(2) Severity level 5, nonperson felony if such items are:

(A) Firearms, ammunition, explosives or a controlled substance that is defined in K.S.A. 2020 Supp. 21-5701, and amendments thereto, except as provided in subsection (b)(3);

(B) Defined as contraband by rules and regulations adopted by the secretary of corrections, in a state correctional institution or facility by an employee of a state correctional institution or facility, except as provided in subsection (b)(3);

(C) Defined as contraband by rules and regulations adopted by the secretary for aging and disability services, in a care and treatment facility by an employee of a care and treatment facility, except as provided in subsection (b)(3); or

(D) Defined as contraband by rules and regulations adopted by the commissioner of the juvenile justice authority, in a juvenile correctional facility by an employee of a juvenile correctional facility, except as provided by subsection (b)(3); and

(3) Severity level 4, nonperson felony if:

(A) Such items are firearms, ammunition or explosives, in a correctional institution by an employee of a correctional institution or in a care and treatment facility by an employee of a care and treatment facility; or

(B) A violation of subsection (a)(5) or (a)(6) by an employee or volunteer of the department of corrections, or the employee or volunteer of a contractor who is under contract to provide services to the department of corrections.

(c) The provisions of subsection (b)(2)(A) shall not apply to the possession of a firearm or ammunition in a parking lot open to the public if the firearm or ammunition is carried on the person while in a vehicle or while securing the firearm or ammunition in the vehicle, or stored out of plain view in a locked but unoccupied vehicle, and such person is either: (1) 21 years of age or older; or (2) possesses a valid provisional license issued pursuant to K.S.A. 75-7c03, and amendments thereto, or a valid license to carry a concealed handgun issued by another jurisdiction that is recognized in this state pursuant to K.S.A. 75-7c03, and amendments thereto.

(d) As used in this section:

(1) "Correctional institution" means any state correctional institution or facility, conservation camp, state security hospital, juvenile correctional facility, community correction center or facility for detention or con-

finement, juvenile detention facility or jail;

(2) "Care and treatment facility" means the state security hospital provided for under K.S.A. 76-1305 et seq., and amendments thereto, and a facility operated by the Kansas department for aging and disability services for the purposes provided for under K.S.A. 59-29a02 et seq., and amendments thereto; and

(3) "Lawful custody" means the same as in K.S.A. 2020 Supp. 21-5912, and amendments thereto.

II. Registered Offender

The persons confined under the KSVPA received a different term of registration under their criminal conviction. Some had a few years, five, years, or lifetime registration requirement. Beginning on July 1, 2001, anyone committed under the KSVPA became required to register for the remainder of their life.

This is an enhancement to their criminal case but the Courts have held it to not be ex post facto or punitive and therefore constitutionally permissible. In addition there is case law that holds a person confined as a sexual predator has a right to clear his name of the title once released, however, this statute ensures that right will never be afforded, for the registration lists the person as a Sexually Violent Predator as a permanent record.

The Kansas Registration Act is long and for this reason is not cited in this book. It can be found at K.S.A. § 22-4901 et seq. The persons confined under the KSVPA did not have to register while in the facility until the Court held that the local Sheriff and the facility was violating the Registration Act by not requiring the SVP's to register. Once the Court ordered the registration to occur, the Sheriff and agency in charge of the facility asked and received a legislative amendment removing a registration requirement while the person is confined in a secure confinement facility under the KSVPA.

It makes sense that a dangerous person would have to register. This is based on the fact that Kansas uses its KORA to show the public all dangerous persons. The dangerousness can be because of a drug or alcohol problem, weapons offense, or being a sex offender or sexually violent predator. Why then do they not require the mentally ill individuals under regular civil commitment to register? They were deemed a danger by the State or another person and confined on this basis, this means they should also be required to register. If not is it a targeted unlawful practice against those under the KSVPA?

III. Battery

The facility the persons confined under the KSVPA are housed in has been around in the State of Kansas for well over one-hundred years. The facility has human workers that work the units and for the entire time the facility has been opened, these humans have been injured, maimed, and disabled by the persons confined therein.

Even though this is true it was not until the year 2006 that the Legislature made it a felony for the confined person. Why is this all of a sudden necessary? A true story is that in the program under the KSVPA there is the least amount of trouble calls and incidents that take place. They are considered the least violent group on campus. In fact there are units where trouble calls and staff getting hurt is almost a daily occurrence. As to those under the KSVPA this appears unnecessary, and under regular civil commitment those confined lack mens rea or ability to control themselves and that is why they are committed, why then charge them?

The statute concerning battery of a mental health employee is K.S.A. § 21-5413.

SEXUALLY VIOLENT OFFENDER

PART III: STATISTICS AND DEMOGRAPHICS

Chapter 1

Introduction

U sing public records available to all citizens I researched the background of three-hundred and forty-three of the men committed under the KSVPA. Yes, I limited it to men because currently there has not been a woman committed as a sexually violent predator in Kansas.

Though there has been more than three-hundred and forty-three, I limited it to this number due to the expense of research and access to information. This number represents no less than ninety (90) percent of those committed as of the year 2022. It provides a very accurate reflection of the overall makeup of those confined under the KSVPA.

Chapter 2

County Statistics

—————⟶∘⟩⟨∘⟵—————

In Kansas there are one-hundred and five (105) counties. Of that number only fifty-eight (58) counties or fifty-five percent (55%), of those have an individual committed to the program based on the review of the three-hundred and forty-three men.

Sedgwick County has committed sixty-six (66) or nineteen point two percent (19.2%) of the three-hundred and forty-three (343).

Wyandotte County has committed sixty-one (61) or seventeen point eight percent (17.8%) of the three-hundred and forty-three (343).

Johnson County has committed thirty-three (33) or nine point six percent (9.6%) of the three-hundred and forty-three (343).

Shawnee County has committed sixteen (16) or four point seven percent (4.7%) of the three-hundred and forty-three (343).

Saline County has committed fourteen (14) or four point one percent (4.1%) of the three-hundred and forty-three (343).

Cowley County has committed twelve (12) or three point five percent

(3.5%) of the three-hundred and forty-three (343).

Butler County has committed nine (9) or two point six percent (2.6%) of the three-hundred and forty-three (343).

Montgomery and Reno County has committed eight (8) or two point three percent (2.3%) of the three-hundred and forty-three (343).

Douglas and Lyon County has committed seven (7) or two point zero percent (2.0%) of the three-hundred and forty-three (343).

Barton County has committed six (6) or one point seven percent (1.7%) of the three-hundred and forty-three (343).

Crawford and McPherson County has committed five (5) or one point five percent (1.5%) of the three-hundred and forty-three (343).

Cherokee, Finney, Geary, Labette and Miami County have committed four (4) or one point two percent (1.2%) of the three-hundred and forty-three (343).

Atchison, Bourbon, Clay, Ford, Harvey, Jefferson, Riley, and Wilson County has committed three (3) or zero point nine percent (0.9%) of the three-hundred and forty-three (343).

Brown, Coffey, Ellis, Ellsworth, Franklin, Leavenworth, Linn, Pawnee, Pratt, Sumner, and Woodson County has committed two (2) or zero point six percent (0.6%) of the three-hundred and forty-three (343).

Allen, Barber, Cloud, Doniphan, Edwards, Graham, Greenwood, Marshall, Mitchell, Morris, Neosho, Osage, Pottawatomie, Rawlins, Rooks, Russell, Scott, Sherman, Stafford, and Washington County has committed one (1) or zero point three percent (0.3%) of the three-hundred and forty-three (343).

CHAPTER 3

STATISTICS OF TREATMENT

The purpose and goal of the KSVPA is rehabilitation and release. If it does not provide treatment then it would be considered an unconstitutional method of confinement. With this in mind we review the statistics of the effectiveness of the treatment. I am using public records and first-hand knowledge to provide the best picture possible, I cannot guarantee the numbers to be one-hundred percent true.

The first striking issue is that there are zero (0) female SVP's in Kansas. This means the State of Kansas has only targeted male offenders for commitment under this scheme;

In treatment there are two tiers in the SPTP facility. After completion of these two tiers the third Tier occurs at a reintegration house. Of the three-hundred and forty-three (343) committed a total of two-hundred and twenty-six (226), fifty-eight percent (58%), are on the first tier (Tier 1) of treatment. Of the three-hundred and forty-three (343) committed a total of forty-two (42), eleven percent (11%), are on the second tier (Tier 2) of treatment. Of the three-hundred and forty-three (343) committed a total of twelve (12), three percent (3%), are on the third tier (Reintegration) of treatment. Of the three-hundred and forty-three (343) committed a total of ten (10), three percent (3%), are on the fourth tier (Transitional Release) of treatment. Of the three-hundred and forty-three (343) committed a total of seventeen (17), five percent (5%), are on the fifth tier (Conditional Release) of treatment.

These statistics show that either the treatment is ineffective or improper, or the individuals are so ill that there may not be treatment available. Either answer begs the question of what is the State spending millions of dollars on? Should more oversight be in place, should changes occur? I am not an expert but as a taxpayer I tend to like to know that my money is being effectively used and not wasted.

CHAPTER 4

AGE STATISTICS

———————⊷○⟪҈⟫○⊶———————

A person's age has been shown to be a determining factor of their risk of recidivism (re-offending). As this is a true factor I reviewed the ages of the three-hundred and forty-three individuals and found the results to be surprising. I will list my detailed findings here and let you deduce your own conclusion concerning it.

The median age at the time of commitment is thirty-eight (38); The median age at the time one reaches reintegration is fifty-eight (58), meaning that one has a minimum of twenty (20) years before he is eligible for reintegration; The median age at the time one reaches transition is sixty-one (61), meaning that one has a minimum of twenty-three (23) years before he is eligible for transition; The median age at the time one reaches conditional is fifty-nine (59), meaning that one has a minimum of twenty-one (21) years before he is eligible for conditional.

The ages show that the program has a goal or intent that one will serve at least twenty years before he can earn any form of pre-release, let alone full release. Though this is not always true, for it is an average, based on the whole it still leads one entering the program to question whether to participate or wait for the time to run. This is an inhibition or block to treatment. This coupled with the statistics of treatment makes the question of should change occur even more interesting.

Chapter 5

Release Statistics

————————⇔○⟨⟋⟍⟍⟍○⇔————————

The State pays an exorbitant amount to confine an SVP in Kansas, in fact it is considerably more than to house them as a prisoner. What is the rate of release for the SVP in Kansas. Using the three-hundred and forty-three individuals and making an average the results might surprise you.

As of the date of the statistical breakdown one person has gained release from the SPTP by completing the program, a total of twenty-seven (27) years after the inception of the program; The program has returned a total number of thirty-five (35), ten percent (10%), residents from reintegration, transitional, or conditional back to secure confinement; a total of fifty-seven (57), seventeen (17%), residents have died while in the program. The median age at time of death is fifty-five (55) years old.

Concerning the forty-seven (47) residents who have gained reintegration, transition, or conditional, of which thirty-five (35) were returned, statistically zero (0) percent re-offended sexually. In fact the main reason for return was due to violating a rule of the reintegration facility. One could ask is this a result of ineffective treatment or overbearing rules with the goal of return in mind. If the goal is to always return the individual to secure confinement this shows residents in the program there is no need to move forward, which in turn thwarts treatment and then the costs rise again.

CHAPTER 6

STATISTICS OF COMMITMENT BY YEAR

—————————⊸o𝓒𝓢⊃o⊶—————————

The KSVPA was enacted in 1994, about twenty-eight years ago. How long have the committed individuals been there? This question can be reviewed by looking at the number of commitments per year of the three-hundred and forty-three individuals.

In 1994 the State committed one (1) individual, or zero point three (0.3) percent. In 1995 the State committed six (6) individuals, or one point seven (1.7) percent. In 1996 the State committed zero (0) individuals, or zero (0) percent. In 1997 the State committed four (4) individuals, or one point two (1.2) percent. In 1998 the State committed eight (8) individuals, or two point three (2.3) percent. In 1999 the State committed eighteen (18) individuals, or five point two (5.2) percent. In 2000 the State committed twelve (12) individuals, or three point five (3.5) percent. In 2001 the State committed seventeen (17) individuals, or five point zero (5.0) percent. In 2002 the State committed twenty-five (25) individuals, or seven point three (7.3) percent. In 2003 the State committed twenty-seven (27) individuals, or seven point nine (7.9) percent. In 2004 the State committed twenty-seven (27) individuals, or seven point nine (7.9) percent. In 2005 the State committed fourteen (14) individuals, or four point one (4.1) percent. In 2006 the State committed nineteen (19) individuals, or five point five (5.5) percent. In 2007 the State committed fifteen (15) individuals, or four point four (4.4) percent. In 2008 the State committed fourteen (14) individuals, or four point one (4.1) percent. In 2009 the State committed seventeen (17) individuals, or five point zero (5.0) percent. In 2010 the State committed sixteen (16) individuals, or four point seven (4.7) percent. In 2011 the State committed eighteen (18) individuals, or five point two (5.2) percent. In 2012 the State committed ten (10) individuals, or two point nine (2.9) percent. In 2013 the State committed eighteen (18) individuals, or five point two (5.2) percent. In 2014 the State committed eleven (11) individuals, or three point two (3.2) percent. In 2015 the State committed fourteen (14) individuals, or four point one (4.1) percent. In 2016 the State committed ten (10) individuals, or two point nine (2.9) percent. In 2017 the State committed seventeen (17) individuals, or five point zero (5.0) percent. In 2018 the State committed six (6) individuals, or one point seven (1.7) percent.

CHAPTER 7

CRIMINAL RECORD STATISTICS

———————⇌o⟨⟩o⇋———————

O f the three-hundred and forty three individuals that information
was received on it is interesting to view their criminal records.
The very idea of a Sexually Violent Predator Act would lead one
to believe these are habitual offenders, but the truth is far far away.

Seven of the three-hundred and forty-three, two percent (2%), individuals do not have a conviction for a sex offense as that term is defined
in the KSVPA. Two-hundred and sixty-two of the three-hundred and
forty-three have only one conviction for a sex offense as that term is defined in the KSVPA. These will be referenced with the term "first time."

Concerning the first timers, twenty-five or ten percent are only
charged with an attempted crime. Forty-six of the first timers, eighteen
percent, remained free from one to five years after their offense before
they were charged. While they were free during those years they did not
commit another offense.

Concerning the first timers, twenty-three, nine percent, were over the age of fifty, and one was seventy, at the time of their offense.

Eighty-one, twenty-four percent, of the three-hundred and forty-three individuals have more than one conviction for a qualifying offense pursuant to the KSVPA.

Five, one percent, of the three-hundred and forty-three individuals were juvenile offenders, meaning they committed their crime before age eighteen.

In reviewing the information the three-hundred and forty-three individuals were placed in a table that had four categories. The first category was Child, where the individual gets a check if the victim was under the age of eighteen. The second category was Adult, where the individual gets a check if the victim was over the age of eighteen. The third category was Rape, this is the original intention of the KSVPA to confine serial rapists. The individual received a check in this box if they had this for a conviction. The fourth category was Habitual, if the individual has two convictions for a qualifying offense under the KSVPA they received a check in this box.

Once the table was created the results were very interesting. Two-hundred and fourteen (214) of the individuals only checked one of the four boxes. This is sixty-two percent (62%) of the three-hundred and forty-three. Ninety-Six (96) of the individuals checked two of the four boxes. This is twenty-eight percent (28%) of the three-hundred and forty-three. Fifteen (15) of the individuals checked three of the four boxes. This is four percent (4%) of the three-hundred and forty-three. Five (5) of the individuals checked four of the four boxes. This is one percent (1%) of the three-hundred and forty-three.

One could say the results of this table show that only one percent (1%) of those three-hundred and forty-three confined under the KSVPA, truly meet the requirement of the intent of the KSVPA. To take this one step further the criminal code in Kansas defines a "habitual offender" as a person, who on or after July 1, 2006, is convicted of a sexually violent crime and has two or more previous convictions for a sexually violent crime.

Concerning the criminal code's definition of "habitual offender" in Kansas only two of the three-hundred and forty-three could be considered eligible under the definition. Two-hundred and sixty-two of the three-hundred and forty-three if release, and somehow caught another sex offense, would still be ineligible to be defined as an "habitual offender" under the criminal code.

It appears that the KSVPA may have intended to only confine serial sex offenders; however, the data available from the State of Kansas shows the exact opposite. Instead it can be said to appear that the State gave a life sentence to a first time sex offender rather than a serial sex offender via application of the KSVPA.

SEXUALLY VIOLENT OFFENDER

PART IV: THE MISMANAGEMENT

CHAPTER 1

INTRODUCTION

I n this part of the book I will discuss issues that directly affect the persons confined under the KSVPA, the public at large, and the tax payers. All information and facts in this part are what I know and may or may not be the whole truth as I am always not allowed to know the truth. What I provide is a firsthand experience as to each issue and what occurred.

The intent and purpose is not to make someone look bad or point fingers, though it may seem that is what the writing shows. I just want the raw information out there, with a little statement of the issues an individual under the KSVPA faces.

I hope this will give rise to some to say, should we be paying for this? Can we as a State not do better? Is this proper or will this lead to massive, expensive litigation? You can be a voice of change to prevent all this from coming to fruition or being worsened. Thank you for reading this.

CHAPTER 2

FIDUCIARY RESPONSIBILITY

———————◁◦⟳◦▷———————

According to recent legislative bills the total cost for the Kansas Sexual Predator Treatment Program (KSPTP) is around twenty-three million ($23,242,652) a year. If we divide by the number of three-hundred and forty-three, as used earlier, this means it costs the State around sixty-eight thousand ($68,000) per person confined each year. This is paid by the taxpayers in Kansas. To determine if this is an appropriate amount we must look to how it is spent.

A. Medication

In the Kansas Department of Corrections an inmate purchases and keeps his own over the counter medications and certain prescribed medication. This is things like Tylenol, vitamins, cold medicine, cough drops, and the like. This allows the inmate to take care of their body and prevent illnesses.

In SPTP the rules are very different. In order to have an over the counter medication the individual must first see a doctor and receive an order (How much is the doctor paid for this service? Enough to drastically increase the cost of Tylenol). After the order is received then the medication room stocks the over the counter medication. In order for the person to receive it he has to ask permission, which comes from a licensed person working in the medication room.

The person working the medication room is a licensed person and draws no less than $18.00 an hour and some are paid almost $50.00 per hour. Normally there is no less than two or three individuals in the medication room. In addition the cost of the medicine under state law has to be purchased after finding the lowest bidder, thus making the cost of the item higher.

It is estimated that the savings on medication alone would be at least $10,000,000.00 per year if the SVP was treated the same as when he was in KDOC. There is no reason to say that the confined SVP cannot be responsible or take care of their own self and medication, it is a control tactic by the facility that costs an exorbitant amount to the taxpayer.

B. Treatment

The treatment within the facility is barely if present at all. Currently the facility has contracted with Sunflower Psychological Services, in Wichita Kansas to provide the licensed therapists that provide the treatment. The problem is that they only average a total of one (1) hour per week of treatment but clock forty hours of work a week.

When I first came to the KSPTP there was a clear outline and treatment schedule. A person had to complete sixteen core courses in order to advance. To do this therapy began at seven AM and ended around 4 PM each day. It was not abnormal for a person to be doing eight hours of therapy per day. The program was set in quarters, every three months a resident would receive new schedule.

A quarter lasted twelve weeks and then there was a week off, known as break week, for the resident to relax and recharge before the next quarter. Today, there are eleven weeks of classes, if led by a therapist and two weeks off. If the class is led by an activity therapist it still goes twelve weeks and then one week off. Thereby allowing the therapists to have two weeks with no scheduled group or class, what are they earning a paycheck for? I cannot say.

Today, however, a person in the program does not have a set outline of classes that has to be completed to advance in treatment. At best he is offered forty-five minutes of group therapy each week and one forty-five minute class. This means his total time in treatment is one-and a half hours per week.

C. Food Service

As with any confined population the State takes on a burden of having to expend funds to feed those it confines. Currently the SPTP program contracts this service out to a company known as Sodexo. The private company is only partly to blame for the exorbitant amount spent.

In 2005 the facility placed residents in the kitchens as workers. This worked well and helped ensure a level of quality and care for the food. In addition the facility collected what was known as Room and Board. Room and Board is a system whereby the facility collects from a person confined some of the costs it expended for confining him. For a Kitchen worker this averaged at least one-hundred dollars a month. On average there was at least twenty kitchen workers, meaning the recoupment for the State was no less than two-thousand dollars a month.

In 2022 the director of the facility decided to remove the VTP workers from the kitchens and have Sodexo solely prepare and send the food to the units. In so doing the director also closed the kitchens in each building and had it set up to where all food is made in the main kitchen, placed in Styrofoam trays, and then delivered, by gas powered vehicle to the building where the individuals live. At the time this occurred Sodexo was paying the wages for the workers from the facility to the State. The rate they were charged was double what the individual made.

Now the State is paying for over two-hundred Styrofoam trays and bowls three times a day. An average cost of this is no less than one dollar and fifty cents. This adds an additional cost of nine-hundred dollars a day, at best figure. Then the loss of income from Sodexo, paying for the workers, for the workers would average to be about five-hundred and forty dollars. The loss of Room and Board is about one hundred and fifty per day. So for closing the kitchen the director adds an additional cost of about sixteen-hundred dollars per day.

The opposite side of this is that there is a foodservice company, why are they not using reusable trays and washing them? The truth is this is what occurred when the individuals in the facility worked in the kitchen, however, it appears that Sodexo does not want to do this and the director of the facility is okay with it.

CHAPTER 3

ESCAPE

A s with any type of confinement escapes are going to happen and unfortunately there has been five in the Kansas Program. However, the first one did not occur until after the program had been open for fourteen years.

A. Number One

The first escape occurred at a Court House in Wyandotte County Kansas. Staff of the facility were ordered to appear with four residents, so the individuals could have their annual review at the court. The facility took the four residents and three staff in one vehicle and made the long drive.

At the court house a staff member needed to use the restroom and left the confined individuals unattended. During this period one resident walked out of the Court House and was free for a few weeks.

B. Number Two

The second escape occurred when the facility placed an individual in a specific building. For this individual he had escaped from this very same building three times in the past. Prior to the escape the individual was vocal about his intent to escape.

This individual befriended a staff member to assist in his escape. This staff member brought him the necessary tools and was in a vehicle parked just outside the facility waiting to give the individual a ride when he escaped. To carry out this escape took a little bit of work and luck.

The individual hid in a laundry cart. It was his hope that the staff would not check the cart and instead just put it outside. The staff did not check the cart and placed it outside with the individual in it. Now the problem is that the individual is in a cart inside a fence that is surrounded by another fence. In addition there are cameras pointed in this area that are being monitored by a security guard for the facility.

The individual climbed out the cart and using the tools the staff member provided him cut through the multiple fences, entered the staff's vehicle and took off. It took several hours before the facility noticed the individual was not present in the facility.

C. Number Three

The third escape occurred when a resident did not return from an outside event. Prior to this the resident had befriended a staff member and received tools and other inappropriate items. On the day he escaped he went to an activity held outside, when the staff brought the individuals in he remained outside. He then cut through a fence and escaped.

The escape was able to occur because staff did not track who went outside and then when coming in track if they brought the same number in that went outside.

D. Number Four

This escape is considered the most brazen and also was the most televised event. The individual who escaped the fourth time remained out for about ninety days. He walked right out the front door.

This individual shaved his beard and cut his hair, then he put on a pair of dress pants and shirt. At the time face masks were required. He got some staff member to let him off the unit by unlocking the unit door and then staff continued to unlock doors until he reached the front exit which was manned by security guards. The security guards did not check the individual, they only assumed that since he was dressed nice and had what appeared to be a cell phone that he was staff, so they opened the door and let him go out.

To aid the escape even further the staff on the unit were not doing the proper safety checks on this individual every thirty minutes as required by the rules of the facility. Therefore, this individual had a minimum of four hours before it was even noticed that he was gone.

E. Number Five

The facility was transporting an individual to a medical appointment. The individual, though fully restrained (Leg restraints, and Belly Chains), decided to walk away from the staff. The staff transporting the individual did nothing to stop him and instead called the local police or sheriff's department to chase down the individual and return him.

F. Corrections Made

The facility has taken strides to improve their response and ability to prevent escape. One of the first things they did was install a security check point out front where all staff entering the facility must pass a metal detector and all belongings are viewed in a Tomography machine. This tomography machine is similar to that used in an airport. This has stopped an individual from receiving tools for escape from a staff they befriend.

They are more vigilant at seeing who is being allowed out of the building, but yet have no way to be one-hundred percent sure. It is still a human post with human error involved. Rather than put in a biometric system to ensure who is leaving, they have chosen to leave the human element.

G. No Offense

The KSVPA is to confine individuals that are so dangerous that without confinement they will sexually re-offend because a mental abnormality or personality disorder causes them to lack control. The escapes from the facility could be used to gauge whether this is true.

Each of the escapes has never led to one re-offending sexually, even when they were free for about ninety days. If the individuals are as dangerous as the State makes out, do you think one would have re-offended sexually? Or is this just proof that there may be those confined under the KSVPA that do not need to be there? An argument could be had for both questions and one should not take this fact lightly.

CHAPTER 4

CONDITIONS OF CONFINEMENT

⟶◦⟨⟩◦⟵

As with any type of confinement there will always be complaints that the conditions of confinement are unbearable or illegal in some fashion. To address this I am going to highlight the most often discussed and raised issues that are discussed within the program. These are the facts as made known to me and are intended to shed light on the issues. You are free based on your own knowledge to make a decision about their lawfulness or appropriateness.

A. Seclusion Disguised as Lockdown

At a detriment to the individuals confined they now institute seclusion, they call it lockdown, at a whim. They do this when someone is walking on campus, a door sensor malfunctions, staff cannot count, or any other reason that makes them feel that a count is necessary. These seclusion periods are not short and at times it can take more than an hour for them to count to thirty individuals on a unit.

In addition they do seclusion when the power goes out. This will occur even if the power goes out in the middle of the night. This is important for at 10:45 PM every night they lock all individuals in their room for the night. In fact once at 1:00 AM the power went out and they went around waking everyone up to do this count. Why would you do this when you locked everyone in about four hours earlier and confirmed they were the one in the room? It was only to be more detrimental to the health and well being of the individuals confined.

Doing seclusion because someone is walking on campus that is suspicious or not known. I do not believe this should occur. Under the laws in Kansas the security guards on campus have the same capacity and authority as a law enforcement officer. As such it makes more sense that they would be called and question the individual rather than placing well over one-hundred people in seclusion.

We also must keep in mind that all periods of seclusion not only interrupt treatment but prevent treatment from occurring as the facility requires that the scheduled treatment not be held during a seclusion period. If the purpose is for treatment and it is being denied due to periods of seclusion that happen no less than once per week, how can it be said that treatment is provided? They also then have the individuals in such a heightened state that the next therapy session is a discussion all about the lockdown, rather than an actual therapeutic task or object.

Some question whether or not the method and manner of seclusion is leading to a Post Traumatic Stress Disorder (PTSD). To discern this we look to how a seclusion period begins. It starts with an announcement over the Public Address system, which is supposed to be for emergencies. The announcement does not always say why the seclusion is in place or who ordered it. In fact more often than not a normal individual does not even know why he was in seclusion. It is only those who wish to spend time researching that can find out why the seclusion occurred.

Now based on the announcement system each time the Public Address system goes off the confined individuals and staff, instantly believe it is to announce another period of seclusion. Keep in mind staff dislike them to, for they then have to do more work than normal, such as bringing ice and water to the rooms, serving meals to the rooms, etc. It sounds like a version of PTSD, will this lead to more diagnosis and more treatment being needed at an additional cost to the state? Time will tell.

B. Constant Illumination

Beginning on or about August of 2012, the facility issued notice that a night light would be turned on in the individual rooms. The light was to remain on from 9:00 PM to 7:00 AM seven days a week. Upon turning the light on the confined individuals and staff noticed it was bright enough to safely read a book by. The staff feared for their jobs and said they would follow the policy.

A short while after this the administration made a change to where the night light was to remain on at all hours of the day. To ensure staff complied with this directive they had the maintenance department remove the switches that allowed the lights to be turned on or off.

There is studies that show being in constant illumination affects a person's health. Even though this was brought to the facility they remain on. It even went to litigation and the Court found no issue. It is a question of whether or not one who can never be in the dark and must always live with fluorescent lights on, will be harmed.

C. State Sponsored Monopoly

In the year 2014 the facility came in with a new policy restricting where individuals confined in the program could spend their money to receive items in the mail. This caused a civil suit to be filed and ultimately the Court held the restriction was lawful.

Prior to the restriction the individuals could order and receive items from anywhere including family and friends. At the time there was not a property department or property officer per se. They also did not have a tomography machine to scan the incoming packages. Since the lawsuit they have a designated property department with designated staff for that department and a Tomography machine to scan all incoming packages. After scanning all packages must be opened in the presence of a property staff member and the contents checked.

With the new measures in place, that should be sufficient, the State via their agents, however, still foster a monopoly. The individuals confined spend thousands of dollars annually, and so do their friends and families. However, only Wal-Mart, Walkenhorst's, Dick Blick, Fire Mountain Gems, Haband, Herrschner's, JJ Games, Keefe, Model Empire, United States Postal Service, and Walgreens can receive profit from these individuals. This appears to be a monopoly and it is state sponsored. What is wrong with Amazon® or Barnes & Noble® or any of the other millions of companies? To my knowledge nothing and with the technology in place one could only get contraband if the staff let it in.

CHAPTER 5

REVIEW OF CONFINEMENT

—————————⌁oᏟᏰᎇ᎒o⌁—————————

The KSVPA requires that the current mental condition of each person confined be evaluated once per year to ensure the confinement lasts no longer than necessary. This was found to be critical to the constitutionality of the KSVPA in Kansas v. Hendricks, 521 U.S. 346, 117 S. Ct. 2072, 138 L. Ed. 2d 501 (1997).

It is true that the State does submit an annual report to the Court each year as the KSVPA dictates. However, what is not known is that the report is only a statement of how the person progressed or digressed in treatment over the year. It is not and does not evaluate the current mental condition of the person.

The provisions of the KSVPA, specifically K.S.A. § 59-29a05(e), require that the person doing an evaluation inform the confined person of the purpose for the evaluation. In accords with this the individual the State has hired to meet the confined individual, begins by informing them that he is only there to evaluate the person's progress in treatment for the year. This cannot lead to determining a valid basis for re-confinement.

Then in an annual review trial the officials of the Program, who testified under oath, stated they would not and do not evaluate the current mental condition of the person ever. They further testified that they would never recommend one for release until they had completed the program as they had designed it. This goes against the decision in Hendricks and allows for an unconstitutional basis to continue confinement.

Some in the public have commented what would occur if the individuals in the program were evaluated. This is a good question, for it would be unknown for currently they are not evaluating the individuals they confined as required by law and the Constitution.

Chapter 6

Education

———————⟡o⟨◯⟩o⟡———————

S tudies have been done that show a confined person that has completed some high school courses has about a fifty-five percent (55%) recidivism rate. If those same individuals have some vocational training it is reduced to thirty percent (30%). If those same individuals receive an associate's degree it lowers to thirteen point seven percent (13.7%). Then it is reduced to five point six percent (5.6%) if they receive a bachelor's degree. It reduces to zero percent (0%) at the receipt of a master's. Article: The Mind Oppressed: Recidivism As A Learned Behavior, 6 Wake Forest J. L. & Pol'y 357.

Does this mean the KSVPA should give a free education to those it confines? The answer is no, however, there is a duty to prepare those it confines for success and to reduce their recidivism risk if/when they are released.

Currently (Year 2022) the facility that confines those under the KSV-PA provides no education abilities. This includes ensuring that one in the program has a High School Diploma or G.E.D. before release. They also provide no vocational skills or training. This should be seen as more harm and not meeting the legitimate governmental interest of helping protect society.

I cannot and will not say the blame is entirely on the facility for why can the individual not seek education on their own? It is true that I have been able to do this and earned some degrees. the problem is that the facility is not open to this and enacts roadblocks to keep it from occurring. The two main roadblocks put up by the program are:

Test Proctor. Most accredited schools require that the final exam be done before a test proctor. This is a person that ensures you are the one doing the test and follow the rules, for example no open book. At times the facility has allowed for this to be done and for their staff to do it and at times they say no. Currently we are in a period where the one in charge does not want to allow for this.

Book sharing to reduce cost. The most expensive part is sometimes the necessary textbooks. I had recently requested the facility allow me to share books with others who were seeking education so we could all reduce our costs. This was met with a firm NO, for the facility has a blanket ban on all borrowing or lending. This means that the costs are more.

To remedy the issue of seeking education I presented a simple plan to the facility and Secretary of KDADS. This was seen as a very positive thing by the therapists and others in the program, however, administration said no and it would be shelved and maybe reviewed later. I am including a copy of this proposal in Appendix A.

Is it permissible to allow an education, a very valid tool in reducing recidivism, to those confined under the KSVPA? Is it not more detrimental to the person than good? Based on your answers you should do all you can based on your answer.

CHAPTER 7

LIFE SKILLS

━━━━━━━━━━━━━━━━━━━⊸०⌒⌒०⊸━━━━━━━━━━━━━━━━━━━

In life there are basic tasks that every person should know how to do. This can include laundry, cooking, responsibility, and computers. As these are basic life skills one would expect the KSVPA and its facility to provide the necessary skills in these areas. However, it is sad to report the exact opposite is true today under the KSVPA. After reading this section you may wonder how the individuals confined there under could even be expected to make it in today's society, and you would be right to think that way.

A. Laundry

A human being wears clothes today and in order to do so an expectation is that they care for them and wash them. Since my introduction to the confinement under the KSVPA the ability to do one's laundry is a privilege with so many rules and restrictions that even if you earn the privilege you may still not be able to wash your clothes.

I have seen individuals leave the program without the ability to do laundry. For me I was raised in a house that taught me this early on, but some were not fortunate. This adds a further burden to the taxpayer in that now the facility has to pay the high costs of having a laundry facility with employees or contracting out the laundry service. In addition they also become responsible for any lost or damaged clothing. This makes no sense to me and it should not be treated as such.

When I was in a juvenile facility they made it clear that each person was to launder their own clothing. The reason was they did not want to be liable and it is a life skill that must be learned. Why then does the KSVPA confinement not do the same you might wonder. Unfortunately I cannot answer this for you.

B. Cooking

A person has to eat. The ability to select, prepare and cook one's own food is important for: (1) It affects their health; and (2) It costs too much to have another do this for you. In the program this has had a varied response.

When I first came into the facility one could grow food in a garden, purchase food from a store, and then had access to a kitchen to prepare and make said food. Then over time it became a privilege. Today it is not even a privilege it is not allowed at all. Because of this individual's have been released and do not even know how to cook. How can they say this is appropriate rehabilitation? Again I cannot answer this and can only say that eventually someone will see the necessity of teaching this very important life skill.

This life skill also can lead to job skills for when an individual is released so it can be said to also be a vocational skill. This meets two necessary components of rehabilitation and its aim or goal to reduce recidivism. The facility has the ability to make this happen, it has been the decision of the administrators to be more punitive than rehabilitative and that is why it is denied.

C. Responsibility

One must be responsible for themselves and have attention to schedules and details. This affects their ability to work and be a productive citizen in society. In the adult prison system and juvenile prison system in Kansas this was recognized. When I was in either place it was on me to be responsible and attend my scheduled work detail, education detail or therapy detail. They did not remind me, escort me, or plead with me to attend.

In the facility this has been varied. At one point we were allowed to do this and travel to and from our scheduled work detail, education detail, therapy detail, or to the yard for exercise. We would sign out so the staff knew where we were and then just go. Slowly over time they eliminated all of this.

Know we have to wait for a staff escort or announcement before we can go anywhere and they must document it or it will lead to seclusion. I call this coddling, like you would do to a child. This trains one to not think or be responsible for themselves and instead to count on mommy and daddy for everything. Therefore once released they expect this to be how it is and struggle with freedom. Why are we doing more damage than rehabilitation?

The answer is that the administrators have no background in therapy and instead either come from a correctional or punitive background, may have been victims themselves, may dislike a sexual predator, or any other unknown reason. Ultimately it can be said that they do not care.

D. Computers

In today's society one will be lost without basic computing skills. This makes it a necessity that these be provided to one in confinement prior to their release. In recognizing this the Kansas Department of Corrections began giving some computer access thirteen years ago (Year 2009) by providing terminals, tablets and e-mail access.

In the facility there are no tablets or e-mail. There are two computers on each unit, a unit has at least thirty residents, the computers are locked down and have no internet. They contain word processing software and a version of Lexis Nexis®. The facility does not provide instruction in how to use the computers or software. In fact when one goes to pre-release (reintegration) they have to immediately begin using the computer and internet, a fact that many struggle greatly with as they have no experience or training.

What should one do and why is this basic life skill not taught to those confined under the KSVPA. I have many years experience in the field of computers and degrees therein and know this can be provided in a safe and effective manner. Based on this I believe this just shows the goal is to be punitive rather than rehabilitative.

PART V: THE POLICIES AND RULES OF THE FACILITY

CHAPTER 1

INTRODUCTION

———————⊸o〰〰o⊶———————

The rules that are applied in the facility are vast. In looking at this the facility is located on the campus of another facility. That facility has its own statutory laws which govern its policies and rules that are different from those under the KSVPA. The Court held that those rules and policies are inapplicable to the one confined under the KSVPA. Merryfield v. Larned State Hospital, 197 P.3d 906, 2008 WL 5428201 (Kan. App. 2008). However, the facility only followed this ruling for a few years and then reverted to applying those rules to those confined under the KSVPA.

The rules when you take both sets are vast, long and too many to fully print or make available. To give you an idea of the rules the SVP lives under some of the more important ones are being included for review. These are true and correct copies as of the time they were placed in this book.

CHAPTER 2

RESIDENT RULEBOOK

<hr>

Aprevious administrator received a copy of the Rule Book from the Department of Corrections and converted it into being the Rule Book for those confined under the KSVPA. The facility titles this as Policy 8.7 Resident Rule Book.

The difference between how it is used in the facility and the Department of Corrections is that the classifications of Rule Violations all carry the same consequences. In the Department of Corrections the classifications affect the level of punishment. This means a Class I is the most severe and receives the harshest penalties and a Class III is the least severe and receives little if any consequences. The Department of Corrections method and manner makes sense.

In bringing this policy in I have left off the cover page, the Table of Contents and the Violation Index. The remainder is a true and correct copy in its entirety.

RULE BOOK INSTRUCTIONS

1. Please review this book and keep it available for reference.

2. You will be notified if there are any changes to this book via e-mail.

3. Suggestions for revising this book must be in writing and submitted to the Program Director-SPTP

4. Reference the "Resident Handbook" for privilege level details and other program information.

5. Reference "SPTP Property Handbook" for property procedures and allowable property.

6. Review SPTP Policy 7.2 Administrative Review.

SECTION 1: CLOTHING, SAFETY, APPEARANCE & LIVING QUARTERS

RULE 1-101 Clothing

A. Each resident shall not wear or have possession of any clothing other than the issued clothing items or those received from an outside source, labeled and belonging to him.

B. Residents are expected to dress appropriately, per the Resident Handbook.

1. Clothes shall fit properly and be non-revealing.

C. Residents are required to wear their identification (ID) badge at all times when not on their unit. The ID badge must be worn in one of two ways on the front of the resident's person and must be easily viewed by staff:

1. Clipped to the upper left chest area.

2. Hanging from an approved "break away" lanyard.

a. Worn around the neck so that the ID is located in the center of the chest area.

b. 18" maximum overall length of lanyard from clasp on back of neck to far end of clip for ID.

c. Clips and clasps are to be plastic only.

NOTE: ID must be worn on the outside of the outermost article of clothing. (i.e. shirt, jacket, etc.)

D. Each resident must follow the program's orders regarding clothing care and handling procedures.

1. If the resident is not authorized to use a washer/dryer, he may not hand launder or solicit the washer/dryer service from other residents.

2. If the resident has medical orders to use the unit washer/dryer, he

may only launder his personal and labeled clothing.

3. If the resident has a medical order to rinse his clothing, he may only rinse his personal clothing returned from the laundry.

4. Clothing labels must be applied by Sexual Predator Treatment Program (SPTP) clothing aides or LSH laundry services.

5. No resident shall purchase laundry products unless authorized to do so.

E. Each violation of this rule (1-101) shall be a Class III offense.

RULE 1-102 Tattoos, Body Markings, and Body Piercings

A. No resident shall place, alter or remove any tattoo or other body marking on the resident's own body or on the body of another resident. The removal or alteration of any tattoo or body marking shall be performed only by a medical order or consult.

B. No resident shall pierce any part of the resident's own body or the body part of any other resident.

C. Each violation of this rule (1-102) shall be a class II offense.

RULE 1-103 Care of Living Quarters (Resident's Room)

A. Each resident shall keep his personal living quarters in a neat, clean and sanitary condition. Clothing shall be neatly hung or stored. Linens shall be exchanged in accordance with the programs established procedures. Basins and toilet bowls shall be kept clean and sanitary.

B. No resident shall alter, paint, or otherwise modify the furniture or equipment located in the resident's personal quarters, or use the furniture and equipment for other than their intended purpose.

C. No resident shall alter or deface the walls, floor, or ceiling of his personal living quarters.

D. Only program issued or purchased furniture, approved in writing, may be used in personal living quarters.

E. Resident may not use program issued or personal linens as furniture coverings, curtains, and/or rugs.

F. Per State and local fire and life safety code, residents must abide by the following:

1. No more than 10% of walls may have wall coverings/wall hangings

2. Nothing is to be hung within 18" of the ceiling/sprinkler head (whichever is lower)

3. There must be 22" of clearance into the room

4. Vents cannot be covered (partially or otherwise)

G. Each violation of this rule (1-103) shall be a class III offense.

RULE 1-104 Use of Safety Devices

A. Each resident shall use the safety devices or equipment as required by the activity or work he is involved in or assigned to.

B. Each violation of this rule (1-104) shall be a class III offense.

RULE 1-105 Unsafe or Unsanitary Practices

A. No resident shall throw trash, rubbish, debris of any kind upon floors, sidewalks, or grounds. All trash, rubbish and debris of any kind shall be placed in the containers provided for that purpose.

B. No resident shall spit or otherwise deposit any other bodily fluids or bodily waste upon the floors, walls, or ceilings of the building, upon sidewalks or grounds. No resident shall collect, smear or throw bodily fluids or wastes.

C. No resident shall smear or throw body waste or fluids or attempt to smear or throw body waste or fluids on any person. It shall not be a defense that the effort to smear or throw the bodily fluids or wastes on or at the other person was unsuccessful.

D. Each violation of Section A (1-105) shall be a Class III violation

E. Each violation of Section B and C (1-105) shall be a Class I violation.

SECTION 2: OWNERSHIP, POSSESSION, REGISTRATION AND USE OF PROPERTY

RULE 2-201 Registration and use of personal property

A. Each resident shall ensure his personal property is properly registered to him by name. Upon any request of any staff, each resident shall, without delay, produce evidence of his ownership, unless the property that is being demanded has previously been reported as lost (see LSH policy AD-19).

1. No resident shall possess property unless the item is properly registered to him.

2. Possession of any property, other than that registered to him, will be cited for violation and returned immediately to the possession of the program until investigation can determine ownership.

3. Resident will be provided a receipt of surrender to the program.

B. Each violation of this rule (2-201) shall be a class II offense.

RULE 2-202 Electronic Personal Entertainment Devices

A. No resident shall possess, play or use an electronic device except as permitted by program policy or procedures.

B. No resident shall play or use an electronic personal entertainment device without ear phone jacks or ear plugs.

C. At no such time should a sound coming from the electronic device exceed the resident's room and personal space. Personal space is defined as three (3) feet within the person.

D. The size, type and capability of the device shall be limited by the decision of the program.

E. Resident may have in his possession only those electronic personal listening devices that are registered to him by program property staff.

F. Each violation of this rule (2-202) shall be a class III offense.

RULE 2-203 Theft

A. Theft shall include, but not be limited to any of the following acts which are done with the intent to deprive the owner of possession, use, or benefit of the owner's property or services:

1. Obtaining or exerting unauthorized control over property or services

2. Obtaining control over property or services by deception

3. Obtaining control over property or services by threat

4. Obtaining control over property or services with the knowledge that the property or services have been stolen by another

B. Each violation of this rule (2-203) shall be a class I offense.

RULE 2-204 Taking Without Permission

A. No resident, regardless of intent, shall take any article of property of any kind from any other person or any place without the expressed permission of the person who is authorized to give such permission.

B. No resident shall obtain articles of property of any kind from any person or any place by fraud or dishonesty.

C. Each violation of this rule (2-204) shall be a class II offense.

RULE 2-205 Unauthorized Dealing and Trading

A. No resident shall trade, barter, borrow, loan, give, receive, sell or buy goods, services, or any item with economic or other intrinsic value with, to, or from another person without the written permission of the Treatment Team or its designee.

B. Each violation of this rule (2-205) shall be a class II offense.

RULE 2-206 Debt Adjustment and Debt Collection Prohibited
        Each of the following acts between and among residents shall
        be prohibited:
1. Debt collection
2. Debt adjustments.
B. Each violation of this rule (2-206) shall be a class II offense.

RULE 2-207 Gambling and Bookmaking
A. No resident shall make any bet, operate, or bank any gambling pool or game, accept or plan any bet of another individual, or engage in any form of gambling.

B. No resident shall possess, transfer, sell, distribute, or obtain dice or any form or type of gambling paraphernalia. Dice may be allowed for accessories to retail games, but must be played only with the game.

C. No resident shall receive, possess, distribute, sell or transfer lottery tickets.

D. Each violation of this rule (2-207) shall be a class III offense.

RULE 2-208 Misuse of state property
A. No resident shall destroy, damage, deface, alter, misuse, or fail to return when due, any article of state property, including clothing and shoes.

B. Each violation of this rule (2-208) shall be a class III offense; additionally, resident will be assessed all costs associated with damage/misuse of state property.

SECTION 3: VIOLENCE, DISRUPTIVE BEHAVIOR AND RIOT
RULE 3-301 Fighting; Violence
A. Each of the following acts shall be prohibited:
1. Fighting;
2. Any act other than fighting that constitutes violence, i.e., pushing,

SEXUALLY VIOLENT OFFENDER

shoving, hitting, or any physical contact
    3. Any act that is likely to lead to violence
    B. Each violation of this rule (3-301) shall be a class I offense

RULE 3-302 Noise
    A. No resident shall utter, vent, or otherwise make any inappropriate booing, whistling, shouting, hissing or catcalls, using profanity, derogatory language or name calling, or any other loud and disturbing noises during programming or non-programming activities or hours.
    B. Each violation of this rule (3-302) shall be a class III offense.

RULE 3-303 Lying
    A. No resident shall lie, misrepresent the facts, mislead, or otherwise give false or misleading information to a staff, clinician, or any other person who is assigned to supervise him or who has a right to obtain information from the resident.
    B. No resident shall make any false or misleading allegations against staff, other resident or any other person.
    C. Each violation of this rule (3-303) shall be a class III offense.

RULE 3-304 Failing to Follow Staff Directive or Redirective
    A. Each resident shall promptly and respectfully follow any staff directive or re-directive, oral or written, or instruction given to him by staff or any other person who is assigned to supervise him. In case of conflicting directives or instructions, the last directive or instruction given shall be followed.
    B. Each violation of this rule (3-304) shall be a class III offense.

RULE 3-305 Insubordination or Disrespect to Staff
    A. Residents are expected to be attentive and respectful towards all staff and each other. Each direct or indirect display of disrespect or argumentation shall be considered insubordination.
    1. A brief, initial exchange or discussion between resident and staff to clarify a directive or re-directive may be permitted if the exchange or discussion is not conducted in an argumentative or disruptive manner, using appropriate language and volume.
    2. Raising one's voice, name calling, pounding on, slamming on/into objects, and making derogatory remarks about the person or the pro-

gram are not considered respectful and will not be accepted.

B. Each violation of this rule (3-305) shall be a class III offense.

RULE 3-306 Threatening or Intimidating Any Person

A. Residents shall not directly or indirectly threaten or intimidate any other person, whether the threat or intimidation is immediate or conditional.

B. An appropriate statement by the resident that he may properly use the legal process to enforce rights or redress wrongs, including the use of the grievance process, shall not be considered a violation of this regulation.

C. Each violation of this rule (3-306) shall be a class I offense.

RULE 3-307 Avoiding Staff

A. At no time should a resident run from, deliberately evade, or otherwise purposefully avoid any staff when required to, directed to, requested to or redirected to be accounted for, be searched or questioned.

B. Each violation of this rule (3-307) shall be a class I violation.

RULE 3-308 Improper Use of Food

A. Residents shall not take or accept more food or beverage than he will consume.

B. No resident shall trade, sell, give away, and barter his food or another resident's food.

C. Residents shall not deliberately destroy food or beverage.

D. Residents shall not carry or otherwise remove any food, food item or beverage; including food items or beverage containers from dining area or kitchen. This includes, but is not limited to: condiments, trays, milk crates, utensils, and napkins for personal or group consumption.

E. All such items found in the resident's possession or outside of the dining area will be destroyed or returned to the cafeteria.

F. Each violation of this rule (3-308) shall be a Class III offense.

RULE 3-309 Misconduct in Cafeteria

A. Each resident shall enter and leave the cafeteria in accordance with the established policy and procedure, and shall act appropriately while in

SEXUALLY VIOLENT OFFENDER

the cafeteria.

B. Residents shall be dressed appropriately for the cafeteria, per established policy and procedure.

C. Each violation of this rule (3-309) shall be a class III offense.

RULE 3-310 Drunkenness, Intoxication, or Altered Consciousness

A. No resident shall be drunk, intoxicated, or in a chemically induced state of altered consciousness at any time.

B. No resident shall brew, concoct, make or possess any alcoholic beverage or substance.

C. An exception shall be any instance of an altered state of consciousness induced by prescribed medications taken in accordance with instructions from and while under the care of qualified medical personnel.

D. Each violation of this rule (3-310) shall be a class I offense.

RULE 3-311 Stimulants, sedative, drugs, or narcotics; misusing or hoarding authorized or prescribed medication

A. No resident shall ingest, inhale, inject, or introduce by any other means any kind of substance into the resident's body or the body of another resident that is capable of producing intoxication, hallucinations, stimulation, depression, dizziness, or any other alteration of the resident's state of consciousness or feeling, except for the following:

1. Approved foods and beverages. Alcohol in any form shall not be deemed an approved food or beverage unless the alcohol is a medicinal ingredient in an authorized or prescribed medication.

2. Any legal drugs, including medication properly and legally prescribed or authorized for the resident by an authorized, licensed physician.

B. The misuse or hoarding of any authorized or prescribed medication shall be prohibited and defined as:

1. Misuse shall mean any use other than that for which the medication was specifically authorized or prescribed.

2. Hoarding shall mean having possession or control of, or holding any quantity of authorized or prescribed medication greater than the amount or dosage that has been issued to the resident by medical staff, or greater than the amount that should be remaining if the resident has taken the medication in accordance with the prescription and instructions from medical staff.

C. Residents, while in possession or control of medication, shall not leave the medical unit or area where the medication is issued, unless the removal of the medication from the unit or area has been authorized in writing by medical staff.

D. Each violation of this rule (3-311) shall be a Class I offense.

RULE 3-312 Sexual Activity; Sodomy

A. No resident shall commit or induce any other person to commit an act of sexual intercourse or sodomy, even with the consent of the other person. Participation in such an act shall be prohibited.

B. No resident shall perform any of the following:

1. Force or intimidate another person to engage in sexual intercourse or sodomy.

2. Solicit or arrange for the application of force or intimidation by another person in order to engage in sexual intercourse or sodomy with another person.

3. Participate in any scheme or arrangement to force or intimidate another person to engage in sexual intercourse or sodomy.

C. Sexual intercourse shall mean any penetration of the female sex organ by a finger, the male sex organ, or any object. Any penetration, however slight, shall be deemed sufficient to constitute sexual intercourse.

D. Sodomy shall be defined as any of the following:

1. Oral contact with or oral penetration of the female genitalia or oral contact with the male genitalia

2. Anal penetration, however slight, of a male or female, by any body part or object

3. Oral or anal copulation between a person and an animal.

E. Each violation of this rule (3-312) shall be a class I offense, and may be a criminal offense per K.S.A. 21-5504.

RULE 3-313 Lewd Acts

A. No resident shall engage in a lewd or lascivious manner in any act of kissing, fondling, touching, or embracing, whether the act is with a person of the same or opposite sex, and whether or not the act is with the consent of the other person.

B. No resident shall intentionally expose a sex organ with the knowledge or reasonable anticipation that the resident will be viewed by others, and with the intent to arouse or gratify the sexual desires of the resident, staff or another individual.

C. Each violation of this rule (3-313) shall be a class I offense.

RULE 3-314 Sexually Explicit Materials (Excluding Authorized Items or Those Items Permitted by Policy and/or the 8.8 Resident Handbook)

A. No resident shall have in his possession or under control any sexually explicit materials, including, but not limited to: books, magazines, drawings, paintings, writings, pictures, items, or devices.

B. Material shall be considered sexually explicit if the purpose of the material is sexual arousal or gratification, or the material meets either of the following conditions:

1. Contains nudity, which shall be defined as the depiction or display of any state of undress in which the human genitals, pubic region, buttock or female breast (at a point below the top of the areola is less than completely and opaquely covered).

2. Contains any display, actually or simulated, or description of any of the following:

a. Sexual intercourse or sodomy, including genital-genital, oral-genital, and anal-oral contact, whether between persons of the same or differing gender

b. Masturbation

c. Bestiality

d. Sadomasochistic abuse

e. Sexually explicit material depicting, describing or exploiting any child under the age of 18 years.

C. Each violation of this rule (3-314) shall be a Class I offense.

RULE 3-315 Disruptive Behavior

A. No resident shall start, solicit, encourage, perform, participate in, or help others to perform or participate in any disruptive behavior.

B. Each violation of this rule (3-315) shall be a Class III offense.

RULE 3-316 Falsifying Documents

A. No resident shall falsify any document.

B. Each violation of this rule (3-316) shall be a Class III offense.

RULE 3-317 Riot or Incitement to Riot

A. No resident shall riot or incite others to riot. Riot shall be defined as either of the following:

1. Any use of force or violence by two or more persons acting together and without authority of law that produces a breach of the peace on the premise, whether within the security perimeter itself or not.

2. Any threat to use the force or violence described by the above paragraph against any person or property, if accompanied by the power or apparent power of immediate execution.

B. Incitement to riot shall be defined as urging others by words or conduct to engage in riot under circumstances that would produce either a clear and present danger of injury to persons or property or a breach of the peace.

C. Each violation of this rule (3-317) shall be a Class I offense.

RULE 3-318 Assault

A. Assault shall be defined as an intentional threat to do bodily harm to another, coupled with the apparent or recognizable ability to carry out the threat and resulting in the other person's immediate apprehension or fear of bodily harm. No bodily contact shall be necessary to complete an assault violation.

B. Each violation of this rule (3-318) shall be a Class I offense.

RULE 3-319 Conduct Regarding Visitors or the Public

A. Residents shall treat all visitors or other members of the public in a respectful and helpful manner.

B. Residents shall maintain a dignified and respectful demeanor while in the presence of these individuals whether in the secured perimeter or not.

C. Each violation of this rule (3-319) shall be a Class II offense.

RULE 3-320 Battery

A. No resident shall commit battery. Battery shall be defined as either of the following:

1. The unlawful or unauthorized intentional touching or application of force to the person or another when done in a rude, insolent, or angry manner.

2. Intentionally or recklessly causing bodily harm to another person.

B. Each violation of this rule (3-320) shall be a Class I offense.

RULE 3-321 Arson

A. No resident shall commit arson.

B. No resident shall own or have in his possession any means of producing fire or an explosive, including but not limited to matches, lighters, lighter fluid, flints, metal strips.

C. Each violation of this rule (3-321) shall be a class I offense.

RULE 3-322 Resident activity; limitations

A. Proselytizing shall be denied as an active effort to persuade any person to convert to a religious faith or belief without the person's prior consent. This does not prohibit a one-to-one conversation about religious matters between two individuals freely participating in the conversation.

B. Each violation of this rule (3-322) shall be a Class III offense.

RULE 3-323 Interference with Restraints

A. No resident shall interfere with or assist or encourage other residents to interfere in any way with restraints that have been, or are being applied to a resident.

B. Each violation of this rule (3-323) shall be a Class I offense.

RULE 3-324 Personal Relationships; Limitations

A. A personal relationship shall be defined as any relationship involving unnecessary familiarity by a resident toward any current or former staff member, volunteer or contract person.

B. No resident shall initiate, solicit, encourage, establish or participate in any type of inappropriate relationship.

C. No resident shall initiate, solicit, encourage, or establish pen pals without prior approval in limited circumstances from the SPTP Program and Clinical Directors.

D. Any contact other than a polite exchange of remarks or casual conversation between a resident and staff shall be limited to that contact necessary to carry out official duties and provide authorized services to the resident in a professional manner.

E. Each violation of this rule (3-324) shall be a Class I offense.

RULE 3-325 Interference with official duties

A. No resident shall intentionally disrupt, sabotage, impede, or interfere with the performance of official duties by any employee or contract staff.

B. Any and all other behavior not specifically addressed herein which is disruptive to the treatment program, other residents, staff or visitors.

C. Each violation of this rule (3-325) shall be a Class II offense.

SECTION 4: BEING PRESENT AND ACCOUNTED FOR

RULE 4-401 Restricted Areas; Unauthorized Presence; Out of Bounds in Assigned Living Area

A. Each resident shall be required to know which areas are designated as restricted areas. No resident shall enter a restricted area without a direct order by an authorized person.

B. No resident shall roam about in the housing unit or be in any place without the permission of an authorized person.

C. Residents may not enter into another resident's room.

D. Residents may not enter into nursing/aide stations.

E. Each violation of this rule (4-401) shall be a Class I offense.

RULE 4-402 Interference with visibility and locking devices

A. No resident shall cover or otherwise obstruct any door, window, passageway, or observation port, including food passage port and slot, in a manner that blocks visibility into the room or space.

B. No resident shall block or otherwise interfere with the opening, closing, or locking of any door or window; including food passage ports and slots.

C. Each violation of this rule (4-402) shall be a Class II offense.

RULE 4-403 Restrictions

A. No resident shall avoid, break or violate the terms of any restriction that has been imposed upon him.

B. Each violation of this rule (4-403) shall be a Class II offense.

RULE 4-404 Medical restrictions

A. No resident shall participate in any program or recreational activities, partake of food or beverage items, or otherwise engage in any activity that is in violation of a documented medical restriction.

B Each violation of this rule (4-404) shall be a Class III offense.

SECTION 5: CONTRABAND

RULE 5-501 Dangerous Contraband

A. Dangerous contraband shall be defined as any of the following:

1. Any item, or any ingredient or part of or instructions on the creation of an item, that is inherently capable of causing damage or injury to persons or property, or is capable or likely to produce or precipitate dangerous situations or conflict, and that is not issued by the program, sold through the canteen, or specifically authorized or permitted for use or possession in designated areas of the program;

2. Any item that can be the basis for a charge of felony for its possession;

3. Any item that, although authorized, is misused if the item in its misused form has the characteristics of being able to cause damage or injury to persons or property or being likely to precipitate dangerous situations or conflicts.

B. All dangerous contraband shall be confiscated and shall be forfeited by the resident.

C. No resident shall possess, hold, sell, transfer, receive, control, or distribute any dangerous contraband.

D. Each violation of this rule (5-501) shall be a Class I offense.

RULE 5-502 Prohibited Items

A. Prohibited items shall be defined as either of the following:

1. Any item, or any ingredient or part of or instructions for the creation of the item, which is not issued by the program, sold through the canteen, or specifically

authorized or permitted for use or possession in designated areas of the program.

2. Any item that, although authorized, is misused in a way that causes some danger or injury to persons or property.

3. For a list of prohibited items, see the Resident Handbook.

B. All prohibited items shall be confiscated and forfeited by the resident.

C. No resident shall possess, hold, sell, transfer, receive, control, or distribute any type of prohibited item.

D. No resident shall possess papers, bottles, containers, trash, or any other item in excess of those limits established by policy or procedure. The possession of excess items described in this section shall be considered prohibited.

E. Each violation of Section B and C shall be a Class I offense.

F. Each violation of Section A shall be a Class II offense.

G. Each violation of Section D (5-502) shall be considered a Class III offense.

RULE 5-503 Tobacco Contraband

A. No resident shall possess, hold, sell, transfer, receive, control, or distribute tobacco products, tobacco substitutes, or smoking paraphernalia, except for as specified in subsection C of this paragraph.

B. For the purposes of this regulation, each of the following terms shall have the meaning specified in this subsection:

1. "Tobacco products" means cigarettes, cigars, pipe tobacco, loose-leaf tobacco, chewing tobacco, and smokeless tobacco. This term shall not include pharmacological aids for smoking cessation approved by the food and drug administration.

2. "Tobacco substitutes" means any substance ingested by smoking, and any herbal or leaf-based replacements for chewing tobacco. This term shall not include any controlled substance.

3. "Smoking paraphernalia" means pipes, lighters, matches, altered batteries, cigarette papers, rolling machines, and all other items fabricated, developed, or processed for the primary purpose of facilitating the use or possession of tobacco products or tobacco substitutes.

C. Residents may engage in bona fide religious activities sanctioned by the program involving the use and possession of tobacco products, tobacco substitutes, and smoking paraphernalia as permitted by and in accordance with the LSH/SPTP policies and procedures.

D. Each violation of this rule (5-503) shall be a Class I offense.

SECTION 6: PUBLISHED LSH/SPTP POLICIES & PROCEDURES

RULE 6-601 Violation of Published Policies & Procedures

A. Unless otherwise stated, each violation of any published LSH/SPTP policy and/or procedure shall be a Class III offense.

SECTION 7: CLASSIFICATION OF OFFENSES AND CONSEQUENCES

RULE 7-701 CLASS I OFFENSES

A. Class I offenses shall be any of the following:

1. Those violations of a very serious nature that are designated in this rule book as class I offenses, whether or not the offenses are also a violation of law.

2. Those violations of law designated by the laws of the state of Kansas.

3. Those violations of law designated by the laws of the United States as felonies.

B. The consequence for a class I offense may be any one or all, or any combination of the following:

1. Restriction status, not to exceed (90) days

2. Restriction from purchasing, not to exceed (90) days

3. Reduction in privilege level

4. Forfeiture of property, not to exceed (90) days, if property item was used in commission of the violation.

RULE 7-702 Class II offenses

A. Class II offenses shall be any of the following:

1. Those violations of moderate seriousness that are designated in this rule book as class II offenses, whether or not the offenses are also a violation of law;

2. Those violations of law designated by the laws of the state of Kansas as misdemeanors

3. Those violations of law designated by the laws of the United States as misdemeanors.

B. The consequence for a class II offense may be any one or all, or any combination of the following:

1. Restriction status, not to exceed (60) days

2. Restriction from purchasing, not to exceed (60) days

3. Reduction in privilege level

4. Forfeiture of property, not to exceed (60) days, if property item was used in commission of the violation.

NOTE: If, within a (90) calendar day period, a fourth (or subsequent) class II violation is committed; the violation is considered a class I.

RULE 7-703 Class III Offenses

A. Class III offenses shall be those violations of a less serious nature that are designated in this rule book as class III offenses, whether or not the offense is also a violation of law. Additionally, each violation of any published policy or procedure that is not otherwise designated in this rule book as a class I or class II offense shall be a class III offense.

B. The consequence for a class III offense may be any one or all, or any combination of the following:

1. Oral or written reprimand

2. Restriction status, not to exceed (30) days

3. Forfeiture of property, not to exceed (30) days, if property item was used in commission of the violation.

4. Reduction in privilege level

NOTE: If, within a (90) calendar day period, a fourth (or subsequent) class III violation is committed; the violation is considered a class II.

RULE 7-704 Consequences for Violating Fast Food Privilege

A. The consequence for violating procedures include:

1. 1st offense – restriction from fast food privileges for (3) months

2. 2nd offense – restriction from fast food privileges for (6) months

3. 3rd offense – restriction from fast food privileges for (1) year

RULE 7-705 Consequences for Violating Movie and Video Privilege

A. A resident found in possession of movies and/or video games identified as prohibited (as referenced in SPTP policy 5.18 and/or the Resident Handbook) will lose the privilege to purchase, receive, possess, or use movies and/or video games for a period of time consistent with the following schedule:

1. 1st offense – (90) calendar days

2. 2nd offense – (180) calendar days

3. 3rd offense – permanently

B. Additionally, any DVD player and/or gaming console (whichever is applicable to the offense) will be confiscated for the period of time indicated on the above schedule.

SECTION 8: DEFINITIONS

Privilege Levels

A. Privilege levels: There are (3) privilege levels within SPTP; Levels A, B, and C, with level A being the highest privilege level and C being the lowest privilege level. Each privilege level determines the privileges, to include some specific property, which a resident can possess.

B. Privilege levels are subject to increase at (90) day increments; the resident is responsible for requesting a privilege level increase – reviews are not done automatically. In order to increase to the next privilege level, the resident must have not been found guilty of any rule violation during the (90) day period. If the resident has been found guilty of a rule violation (regardless of the class), the (90) day period starts from the last conviction date. Residents are only afforded the privileges, and some specific property, that coincide with that privilege level; therefore, a reduction in privilege level will result in loss of privileges and some specific property (allowed by privilege level). Refer to the Resident Handbook for more specific privilege level information.

Restriction Status
A. Restriction status means the following:
1. The Resident will eat trays on the unit
2. The Resident will have fresh air breaks, which (in most cases) will consist of two (2) per day and each break will be directly supervised by staff in a designated area.
3. The Resident IS NOT allowed to participate in any "open" activities
4. The Resident is restricted to the unit, with the exception of scheduled programming/religious activities and medication line.
5. The resident is to be in his room by 2200 hours (10:00 pm) each night, no exceptions; room door will be locked (per K.S.A. 59-29a22, B, iii), and unlocked at 0530 hours (5:30 am).

Restriction from purchasing; and Specific property restrictions.
A. The resident is prohibited from making any type of purchases, except for the following:
1. Medically necessary items, as indicated by medical staff
2. Items necessary for religious practice, as determined by the chaplain
3. Phone minutes
4. Stamps/Postage
5. Necessary legal material
B. The program/unit will provide the resident with basic hygiene necessities during the restriction period.

CHAPTER 3

GRIEVANCE PROCESS

T he next policy is the internal grievance process. The facility titles it as Policy 7.1 Resident Grievance Process. This governs the start of administrative remedies for one confined under the KSVPA. In bringing this one I have left off the title bar, reference section, signature bar, and previous version dates. This is one of several administrative remedies available in the facility.

PURPOSE

To clearly define the procedures that govern the Sexual Predator Treatment Program (SPTP) Resident Grievance Process.

POLICY

The grievance policy provides residents with a process in which to grieve issues within the SPTP.

I. Computation of Timelines

A. For the purpose of this policy, the first day being counted and triggering timelines is the first working day following receipt of the documents.

B. Definition of Working Day: Monday through Friday 8:00 a.m. -5:00 p.m. excluding holidays recognized by the State of Kansas.

C. At each stage, all grievances should be responded to in a timely manner to ensure that delay will not impose additional hardship on the resident or unnecessarily prolong a misunderstanding.

II. Grievances by Residents

A. Prior to utilizing the outlined grievance process, residents are encouraged to attempt to reach an informal resolution of the matter with the staff who work with the resident on a direct or daily basis including but not limited to Mental Health / Developmental Disability Technician (MHJDD), Shift Leader, Registered Nurse (RN), Primary Therapist, or Unit Leader.

B. The grievance process incorporates two levels of problem solving to ensure solution at the lowest administrative level possible.

Note: Residents are required to exhaust this internal SPTP grievance process before the filing of action in the Office of Administrative Hearings or the district court under K.S.A. § 59-29a24.

C. Each resident will be allowed to complete a grievance. The process will be made accessible to mentally impaired and physically handicapped residents by the unit staff, Treatment Team, or SPTP Program Director/Designee.

D. The grievance process shall be applicable to a broad range of matters that directly affect residents, including, but not limited to:

1. Complaints by residents regarding policies and conditions within the jurisdiction of the SPTP.

Actions by employees and residents and incidents occurring within the facility.

E. The grievance process shall not be used in any way as a substitute for, or as part of, the administrative review process outlined in SPTP Policy No.: 7.2 -Administrative Review, SPTP Policy No.: 7.3 -Administrative Review of Treatment Tiers, SPTP Policy No.: 8.6 -Denial or Restriction of a Resident Right, or LSH Policy AD-19.0 Personal Injury or Property Damage or Loss, Including Lost/Missing Laundry Claims.

F. Emergency Grievances

1. "Emergency grievances" shall mean those grievances for which disposition according to the regular time limits would subject the resident to

a substantial risk of personal injury or cause other serious and irreparable harm to the resident. "Irreparable harm" for the purposes of this policy is a harm which cannot be remedied unless corrective action is immediately taken.

2. The resident shall indicate on the face of the grievance form the nature of the emergency and shall write the word "emergency" at the top of either Resident Grievance Process Steps I and II or Resident Grievance Process Steps III and IV.

3. Emergency grievances shall be forwarded immediately, without substantive review, to the level at which corrective action can be taken. Emergency grievances shall be expedited at every level. The same external review provisions that apply to regular grievances shall apply to emergency grievances.

4. If the person at the corrective action level determines that the grievance is not an emergency, the an explanation of the determination shall be included on either Resident Grievance Process Steps I and II or Resident Grievance Process Steps III and IV and said form shall be signed by the person who made that determination and returned to the resident to file through the standard grievance process.

PROCEDURE
III. Forms and Retention
    Forms
Resident Grievance Process forms shall be made available to all residents on the unit computers.

2. If a resident would like to have copies of supporting documentation, they would need to utilize their copy card pursuant to SPTP Policy No.: 5.11 -Copies for Residents. Residents determined to be indigent in accordance with SPTP Policy No.: 8.3 -Resident Mail, shall be allowed up to fifteen (15) copied pages per month.·

3. Page Limitations
    a. At each step of the grievance process, the total number of pages of resident grievance text shall not exceed four (4) pages.
    b. Text appearing on the front and back of a page shall count as two (2) pages.
    c. Any page of text beyond (4) four pages shall not be considered

when determining the merits of the grievance.

d. Resident grievances are to be written legibly if handwritten.

e. If the grievance is not legible, it will be returned to the resident to correct. The resident will be given two (2) working days to resubmit the grievance if desired.

f. If typewritten, the font shall be eleven point or larger and double-spaced.

4. No Adverse Action

a. No adverse action shall be taken against any resident for use of the grievance process unless the resident uses the grievance process for any of the above mentioned purposes, and in those instances the program will consider taking appropriate action against the resident, which could include issuing a notification and/or referring the matter to Safety/Security.

b. No adverse action shall be taken against any employee for good faith participation in the grievance process.

B. Records Retention

Records include forms and supplemental documentation submitted with grievances.

Records shall be collected and maintained systematically by SPTP. These records will be preserved for at least three years following final disposition of the grievance, at which time they will be archived.

Records regarding an individual's participation in grievance proceedings shall be considered confidential and shall be handled under the same procedures used to protect other confidential case records. Consistent with ensuring confidentiality, members of the staff who are participating in the disposition of a grievance shall have access to records essential to the resolution of the grievance. This, however, shall not permit review of grievances submitted by other residents. Grievance records shall not be placed in the resident's medical file.

Note: At each stage of the grievance process, the grievance is delivered to the SPTP Due Process Coordinator/Designee who will log and process the grievance for record keeping purposes. The SPTP Due Process Coordinator/Designee has two (2) working days to complete this process prior to the grievance going through the levels of the procedures.

IV. Grievance to the SPTP Due Process Coordinator Grievance Officer !Designee:

A. Submission: Residents must submit grievances within fifteen (15) working days from the date of the discovery of the event giving rise to the grievance. No grievance, regardless of time of discovery, shall be submitted later than six months after the event.

1. Late Submissions: Any grievance submitted later than these deadlines may be returned to the resident without investigation. Returned grievances shall be assigned a case number, note the name of the individual returning the grievance, the date of the return, and the reasons for the return.

2. Abuse: No resident shall abuse the grievance process by repeatedly submitting the same complaint without allowing the Due Process Coordinator/Designee the opportunity to sufficiently investigate the original grievance as permitted in this policy.

a. Repeated submissions shall be returned to the resident without further substantive response.

b. No resident shall use the grievance process for any of the following purposes: 1) To communicate a threat to another person or the security of the facility. 2) To make a complaint knowing that it is false, malicious, or made in bad faith. 3) To commit any unlawful act.

B. The resident completes the Resident Grievance Process Steps I and II Form LSH343c, which shall include the following information:

A specific complaint that states what or who is the subject of the complaint, related dates, locations, and what effect the situation, problem, or person is having on the resident that makes the complaint necessary.

2. The policy or rule that is implicated.

3. The action that the resident wants the SPTP Due Process Coordinator/Designee to take to solve the problem.

4. The resident's signature and date on which the completed Resident Grievance Process Steps I and II Form was delivered to a unit staff member for transmittal to the SPTP Due Process Coordinator/Designee.

C. The staff member shall sign and date the Resident Grievance Process Steps I and II Form upon receipt from the resident and forward it to the SPTP Due Process Coordinator/Designee for processing within three (3) working days.

D. SPTP Due Process Coordinator/Designee's Response:

1. The Resident Grievance Process Steps I and II form shall be returned to the resident, with a response, within fifteen (15) working days

from the date of receipt.

2. Each response shall include the SPTP Due Process Coordinator/ Designee's findings of fact, conclusions made, and actions taken, as well as, the SPTP Due Process Coordinator/Designee's signature and date completed. All allegations in each grievance will be investigated and if it appears a resident or employee is involved in the matter, they shall not participate in the resolution of the grievance.

3. In all cases, the original and one copy of the Resident Grievance Process Steps I and II shall be returned by the SPTP Due Process Coordinator/Designee to the resident upon receipt of the resident's signature and date.

4. A second copy of the completed Resident Grievance Steps I and II Form shall be retained by the SPTP Due Process Coordinator/Designee.

V. Appeal to the SPTP Program Director/Designee:

A. If the SPTP Due Process Coordinator/Designee answer does not resolve the grievance, the resident may appeal to the SPTP Program Director/Designee by indicating on the Resident Grievance Process Steps III and IV Form LSH-344c what action the resident believes the SPTP Program Director/Designee should take. The resident must sign and date Resident Grievance Process Steps III and IV Form upon submission. The resident's appeal must be made within three (3) working-days of receipt of the SPTP Due Process Coordinator/Designee's decision or within three (3) calendar days of the deadline for that decision, whichever is earlier.

B. The Resident Grievance Process Steps III and IV Form will be given to unit staff member who will sign and date and subsequently deliver the appeal to the SPTP Due Process Coordinator/Designee.

C. SPTP Due Process Coordinator/Designee will sign and date the Resident Grievance Process Steps III and IV Form and cause it to be recorded and sent to the SPTP Program Director/Designee. Page 6 of7

D. When an appeal of the SPTP Due Process Coordinator/Designee's decision is made to the SPTP Program Director/Designee, the SPTP Program Director/Designee shall have twenty (20) working days from receipt to return the Resident Grievance Process Steps III and IV form to the resident with an answer. The answer shall include the SPTP Program Director/Designee's findings of fact, conclusions made, and actions taken, as well as, the SPTP Program Director/Designee's signature and date. All allegations in each grievance will be investigated and if it appears a resident or employee is involved in the matter, they shall not participate in the resolution of the grievance.

E. The resident must sign and date upon final receipt of the completed Resident Grievance Process Steps III and IV Form.

F. If a Resident Grievance 'Process Steps III and IV Form is submitted to the SPTP Program Director/Designee without prior action by the SPTP Due Process Coordinator/Designee, the Resident Grievance Process Steps III and IV Form may be returned to the SPTP Due Process Coordinator/Designee provided the issue is not deemed emergent. If the SPTP Due Process Coordinator/Designee did not respond in a timely manner, the Resident Grievance Process Steps III and IV Form shall be accepted by the SPTP Program Director/Designee and responded to.

VI. Appeal to the Office of Administrative Hearings

A. You may appeal this final agency determination by filing within thirty (30) days a request for hearing in writing with the office of administrative hearings for a review of the determination. Proceedings shall be governed under the Kansas administrative procedure act. Any request for hearing must be accompanied by a copy of the final agency determination, including all documentation submitted in the LSH case number and all agency responses.

B. Failure to timely request a hearing constitutes a waiver of the right to any review. You may have legal counsel represent you at the hearing at your expense. If you wish to request a hearing, you may do so by completing and sending the Request for Administrative Hearing form and a copy of the final agency determination, including all documentation submitted in the LSH case number and all agency responses to: Office of Administrative Hearings Director 1020Kansas Avenue, Topeka, KS 66612-1327

C. Failure to file a written request for hearing accompanied by a copy of the final agency determination with the office of administrative hearings within thirty (30)' days constitutes waiver of the right to any review of the final agency determination.

D. You may obtain a SSP/SPTP Request for Administrative Hearing form on your unit.

CHAPTER 4

LOSS OF TIER REVIEW

The next policy is the internal administrative review policy for tier reassignment. The facility titles it as Policy 7.3 Administrative Review of Treatment Tiers. This governs the start of administrative remedies for one confined under the KSVPA. In bringing this one I have left off the title bar, reference section, signature bar, and previous version dates. This is one of several administrative remedies available in the facility.

PURPOSE
To clearly define the procedures that shall govern an administrative review of:
1. Tier re-assignment, and
2. Return from a reintegration facility to Lamed State Hospital (LSH) Sexual Predator Treatment Program (SPTP).

POLICY

This administrative review policy and procedure explains the process afforded to residents to request and receive administrative review of a treatment Tier re-assignment and/or return from a reintegration facility.

PROCEDURES

I. Computation of Timelines

A. For the purpose of this policy, the first day being counted is the first working day following receipt of the documents.

B. Definition of Working Day: Monday through Friday, 8:00am 5:00pm, excluding holidays recognized by the State of Kansas.

C. All deadlines established in this policy are subject to an extension being granted by the Program Director/Designee. A resident may request an extension in writing to the Hearing Officer/Designee using the Resident Request Form -SPTP-30 and attach a copy to the appropriate appeal form. Extensions for the Hearing Officer/Designee or Program Director/Designee may be granted. When additional time is needed to adequately and appropriately investigate the matter, conduct any necessary witness interviews, hold any necessary hearings, or to allow a reasonable period of time for review. The extension deadline will be documented on the Appeal to the Hearing Officer form -LSH-341c or Appeal to the Program Director form -LSH-366c.

II. Tier Re-Assignments

A. Steps in the Process:

Before a Tier re-assignment is recommended, the Tier reduction process explained below should be used.

1. The resident is informed that the resident's behavior(s) and/or participation in treatment is not consistent with the criteria associated with the Tier to which the resident is currently assigned and the resident shall be given a period of time coinciding with the review of the resident's Comprehensive Integrated Treatment Plan (CITP) to meet a defined and outlined treatment plan. During this time period, the resident must demonstrate that the resident meets the criteria associated with their current Tier assignment. This process is documented in the resident's CITP.

2. If the determination of the Treatment Team is to re-assign the resident to a lower Tier, the Treatment Team will submit a written explanation of the proposed reassignment to the resident, stating the reasons for the reduction. The resident may choose to either accept this re-assign-

ment or request administrative review by an impartial Hearing Officer.

B. Appeal to the Hearing Officer

1. If the resident wishes to request a review, then the resident must complete the Appeal to the Hearing Officer Form -LSH-341c and submit it within two (2) working days to their Treatment Team.

2. When the Treatment Team receives a completed appeal form indicating the resident's intent to request an administrative review:

a. The Appeal to the Hearing Officer form and relevant materials will be forwarded to the SPTP Administrative Assistant, who will log the form and assign a tracking number.

3. A Hearing Officer, who is a clinical supervisor, will then be assigned by the SPTP Program Director/designee to conduct this review. This Hearing Officer will be someone not currently a member of nor directly supervisory over the resident's current Treatment Team.

a. The Hearing Officer shall initiate a review after receiving the resident's request. This review may consist solely of an examination of the resident's CITP and/or other records and interviews with any appropriate person(s).

b. If the Hearing Officer determines that it is helpful to them to do so, the Hearing Officer may meet with the resident face-to-face in order to give the resident an opportunity to be heard and/or the Hearing Officer may allow the resident to present any other written evidence the resident wishes to have considered.

c. If the resident feels they are incapable of representing themselves in this matter they may submit a request to the Treatment Team for the appointment of a staff member to speak on their behalf.

d. If the Hearing Officer concurs or determines on their own that the resident is incapable of representing themselves, then the Hearing Officer shall ask that a staff member be appointed to speak on the resident's behalf. That staff member will be assigned by the SPTP Program Director/designee from staff from outside of that Treatment Team and that staff member will follow through on behalf of the resident for the duration of that specific review.

4. The Hearing Officer will render a written decision within ten (10) working days after receipt of the resident's request for a review and shall state the reasons for the Hearing Officer's determination(s). The Hearing Officer may uphold the proposed Tier re-assignment, may reverse that

determination, or may remand that determination back to the Treatment Team for further consideration and review, and with a requirement that the proposed Tier re-assignment shall be resubmitted to the Hearing Officer by a specified date.

a. The Hearing Officer's decision shall be delivered to the Treatment Team/designee.

b. The Treatment Team/designee will then inform the resident of the Hearing Officer's decision, usually within two (2) working days after receiving the Hearing Officer's decision.

c. If the Hearing Officer decision upholds the Treatment Team's recommendations, the resident shall be re-assigned to the proposed lower Tier. If not, the resident shall remain assigned at their current Tier.

C. Appeal to the Program Director

1. If the resident wishes to appeal the decision of the Hearing Officer they must complete the Appeal to the Program Director Form -LSH 336c within two (2) working days of receipt of the Hearing Officer's decision having been given to them by the Treatment Team/designee. The resident's appeal must clearly state the reason(s) why they believe the Tier re-assignment to be incorrect.

2. The resident's appeal shall be referred to the SPTP Program Director.

3. The resident must submit any new evidence or arguments in writing. The resident's appeal must be typewritten or be clearly printed or legibly written. If a resident's appeal is not legible, it shall be returned to the resident so noted and the resident shall then have two (2) working days to resubmit the appeal in a clearly legible fashion. If the resident fails to do so, the appeal shall be summarily denied.

4. The SPTP Program Director shall consider whether the resident's submission constitutes new, relevant, and pertinent evidence or a valid argument against the reasons for the proposed Tier re-assignment. The SPTP Program Director will render a written decision within ten (10) working days of receipt of the appeal to the Program Director.

a. If the resident's submission does not constitute new, relevant, and pertinent evidence or a valid argument against the reasons for the proposed Tier re-assignment and the Hearing Officer's decision is consistent with program policy, the appeal shall be denied.

b. If the resident's submission does constitute new, relevant, and pertinent evidence or a valid argument against the reasons for the proposed Tier re-assignment the SPTP Program Director/Designee shall overturn the Hearing Officer's decision. If the SPTP Program Director/Designee overturns the Hearing Officer's decision, the SPTP Program Director/Designee may-schedule an informal meeting with the resident, or with the resident and the Hearing Officer. The SPTP Program Director/Designee's decision could result in:

i. A new review by the Hearing Officer or a new Hearing Officer, and a new decision, or

ii. A reversal of the Treatment Team's proposed (initiated)Tier reassignment and reinstatement of the resident to his previous Tier.

D. The SPTP Program Director/Designee's final decision shall be communicated to the Treatment Team/designee, who shall then convey that decision to the resident usually within two (2) working days after receipt of the SPTP Program Director/Designee's decision.

E. Within the administrative review process, as described herein, the SPTP Leadership Team reserves the right to amend these procedures dependent on previously unforeseen emerging situations occurring outside of the ordinary process described herein. The SPTP Program Director will provide written documentation explaining the previously unforeseen emerging situation dictating the need for any amendment. This documentation will accompany the paperwork concerning the particular review throughout the rest of the process.

III. RETURNS TO LSH (SPTP) FROM A REINTEGRATION FACILITY:

Steps in the Process:

A. Notification Report

1. Any resident at a reintegration facility whose behaviors and/or participation in treatment is not consistent with the criteria associated with the reintegration program to which they are currently assigned and/or has become a risk to the public may be subject to an immediate return to SPTP on the LSH campus. In order for a return to occur, except in a situation of extreme risk of harm being committed upon a reintegration facility staff member or other persons, or of escape by the resident, necessitating immediate return of the resident to LSH, the reintegration facility staff must have presented the resident's circumstances to the Progress Review Panel (PRP) for their review. The PRP shall determine

whether or not the resident shall be returned to LSH.

2. Such immediate transfers may be made for therapeutic, safety, and security reasons such as situations involving imminent or on-going danger to self, staff, other residents, and/or the general public. In the event that an administrative review, as provided for herein, ultimately determines that the immediate return to the SPTP was inappropriate, the resident shall be returned to their prior reintegration program and the appropriate facility.

a. Due to security concerns associated with this type of reduction and subsequent return from the reintegration facility to LSH, the resident may not be informed of their impending return to LSH until such time that LSH transport has been dispatched to return said resident. This process is documented in the resident's medical record at the reintegration facility, and their CITP upon arrival to LSH.

b. Prior to departure from the reintegration facility, reintegration facility staff, in consultation with the PRP, will present the resident with a written Notification Report, to notify the resident of the impending return to LSH (SPTP) and the reasoning/rationale for such a decision.

i. Upon notification at the reintegration facility, the resident may choose to immediately accept this return, immediately request an administrative review by an impartial Hearing Officer in the SPTP at LSH, or may delay their decision for two (2) working days as to whether or not they accept or wishes to appeal their return.

ii. It should be noted that the return from the reintegration facility to the SPTP at LSH will occur regardless of the immediacy of the request for a review. Administrative review will occur in the SPTP at LSH. The resident may submit an Appeal to the Hearing Officer Form -LSH-341c. Additionally, upon a resident's return from the reintegration facility, the resident's Tier and Privilege Level assignment at LSH (SPTP) will be determined by the resident's assigned Treatment Team. The resident will be given notice of those assignments and will have the right to either accept the assignments or request an review of either or both of the assignments by following the procedures provided within this policy in Sections I, II, or III, as appropriate.

B. Appeal to the Hearing Officer

1. If the resident wishes to request a review of their return from the reintegration facility to LSH (SPTP), then the resident must complete the Appeal to the Hearing Officer Form -LSH-341c and submit it within two

(2) working days to their Treatment Team at LSH (SPTP).

2. When the Treatment Team receives a completed appeal form indicating the resident's intent to request an administrative review:

a. The completed Appeal to the Hearing Officer form and relevant materials will be forwarded to the SPTP Administrative Assistant, who will log the form and assign a tracking number.

b. A Hearing Officer will then be assigned. This Hearing Officer will be an impartial person not previously involved with this specific incident and shall not be a member of the resident's current Treatment Team. The administrative review shall be presented to the Hearing Officer usually within two (2) working days of the resident's request.

i. The Hearing Officer shall initiate a review after receiving the resident's request. This review may consist solely of an examination of the resident's chart and/or other records and interviews with any appropriate person(s).

ii. If the Hearing Officer determines that it is helpful to them to do so, the Hearing Officer may meet with the resident face-to-face in order to give the resident an opportunity to be heard and/or the Hearing Officer will allow the resident to present any other written evidence the resident wishes to have considered.

If the resident feels they are incapable of representing themselves in this matter they may submit a request to the Treatment Team for the appointment of a staff member to speak on their behalf.

iii. If the Hearing Officer concurs or determines on their own that the resident is incapable of representing themselves, then the Hearing Officer shall ask that a staff member be appointed to speak on the resident's behalf. That staff member will be assigned by the SPTP Program Director/Designee/designee from staff from outside of that Treatment Team and that staff member will follow through on behalf of the resident for the duration of that specific review.

3. The Hearing Officer will render a written decision usually within ten (10) working days after receipt of the resident's request for a review and shall state the reasons for the Hearing Officer's determination(s). The Hearing Officer may uphold the return from the reintegration facility to LSH (SPTP) or may reverse that determination.

4. If the Hearing Officer finds that appropriate reasoning/rationale has been provided by the PRP in their determination to return the resident from the reintegration facility to LSH (SPTP), the Hearing Officer

shall affirm the return. The hearing officer should not merely substitute their judgment as to whether the resident should have been returned to LSH (SPTP) for that of the Progress Review Panel.

5. The Hearing Officer's decision shall be delivered to the Treatment Team/designee.

a. The Treatment Team/designee will then inform the resident of the Hearing Officer's decision, usually within two (2) working days after receiving the Hearing Officer's decision.

b. If the Hearing Officer decision upholds the return from the reintegration facility to the SPTP at LSH, the resident shall remain in the SPTP at LSH. If not, the resident shall return to the reintegration facility.

C. Appeal to the Program Director

1. If the resident wishes to appeal the decision of the Hearing Officer they must complete the Appeal to the Program Director Form -LSH-336c within two (2) working days of receipt of the Hearing Officer's decision having been given to them by the Treatment Team/designee. The resident's appeal must clearly state the reason(s) why they believe the return from the reintegration facility to LSH (SPTP) to be incorrect.

2. The resident's appeal shall be referred to the SPTP Program Director/Designee.

3. The resident must submit any new evidence or arguments in writing. The resident's appeal must be typewritten or be clearly printed or legibly written. If a resident's appeal is not legible, it shall be returned to the resident so noted and the resident shall then have two (2) working days to resubmit the appeal in a clearly legible fashion. If the resident fails to do so, the appeal shall be summarily denied.

4. The SPTP Program Director/Designee shall consider whether the resident's submission constitutes new, relevant, and pertinent evidence or a valid argument against the reasons for the instituted return from the reintegration facility to the SPTP at LSH. The SPTP Program Director/Designee will render a written decision usually within ten (10) working days of receipt of the resident's request for a review.

a. If the resident's submission constitutes new, relevant, and pertinent evidence or a valid argument against the reasons for the instituted return from the reintegration facility to the SPTP at LSH and the Hearing Officer's decision is consistent with program policy, the appeal shall be denied.

b. If the resident's submission constitutes new, relevant, and pertinent evidence or a valid argument against the reasons for the instituted return from the reintegration facility to the SPTP at LSH, the SPTP Program Director/Designee shall overturn the Hearing Officer's decision. If the SPTP Program Director/Designee overturns the Hearing Officer's decision, the SPTP Program Director/Designee may schedule an informal meeting with the resident, or with the resident and the Hearing Officer. The SPTP Program Director/Designee's decision could result in:

i. A new review by the Hearing Officer or a new Hearing Officer, and a new decision, or

ii. A reversal of the initiated return from the reintegration facility to LSH (SPTP) and reinstatement of the resident to his previous Tier.

D. The SPTP Program Director/Designee's final decision shall be communicated to the Treatment Team/designee, who shall then convey that decision to the resident usually within two (2) working days after receipt of the SPTP Program Director/Designee's decision. If a return to the reintegration facility is determined, both the Director of the reintegration facility and the PRP will be notified.

E. Within the administrative review process, as described herein, the SPTP Leadership Team reserves the right to amend these procedures dependent on previously unforeseen emerging situations occurring outside of the ordinary process described herein. The SPTP Program Director/Designee will provide written documentation explaining the previously unforeseen emerging situation dictating the need for any amendment. This documentation will accompany the paperwork concerning the particular review throughout the rest of the process.

F. Appeal to the Office of Administrative Hearings

1. YOU MAY APPEAL this final agency determination by filing within thirty (30) days a request for hearing in writing with the Office of Administrative Hearings for a review of the determination. Proceedings shall be governed under the Kansas administrative procedure act. Any request for hearing must be accompanied by a copy of the final agency determination, including all documentation submitted in the LSH case number and all agency responses.

2. Failure to timely request a hearing constitutes a waiver of the right to any review. You may have legal counsel represent you at the hearing at your expense. If you wish to request a hearing, you may do so by completing and sending the Request for Administrative Hearing form and

a copy of the final agency determination, including all documentation submitted in the LSH case number and all agency responses to: Office of Administrative Hearings Director 1020 S. Kansas Avenue, Topeka, KS 66612-1327.

3. Failure to file a written request for hearing accompanied by a copy of the final agency determination with the Office of Administrative Hearings within thirty (30) days constitutes waiver of the right to any review of the final agency determination.

4. You may obtain a SSP/SPTP Request for Administrative Hearing form on your unit.

CHAPTER 5

RIGHTS RESTRICTION

The next policy is the internal process for restricting a right of one confined under K.S.A. § 59-29a22. The facility titles it as Policy 8.6 Denial or Restriction of a Resident Right. In bringing this one I have left off the title bar, reference section, signature bar, and previous version dates. This is one of several administrative remedies available in the facility.

This policy is the most challenged within the facility for it sets no enforceable time limits on the staff to carry out their duties, but it does for the confined person. Currently the individuals have and are waiting several years for the staff to carry out their duties under this policy if they carry them out at all.

PURPOSE

To clearly define the procedures affording due process for the denial or restriction of a resident's right(s) under KS.A. 59-29a22(b)(15)-(22), including but not limited to, the right(s) to: (1) send and receive non-legal, non-official, or non-privileged mail, (2) phone use, (3) clothing, (4) personal possessions, (5) individual storage space, (6) privacy in toileting and bathing, (7) visitation, (8) presentation of grievances, (9) communicate with public officials without justifiable fear of reprisal, and (10) spend money.

POLICY

This Denial or Restriction of a Resident Right policy establishes a procedure to afford residents an opportunity to request and receive due process when a resident's right(s), as provided in KS.A. 59-29a22(b)(15)-(22), are denied or restricted.

PROCEDURE

Participating members include: Due Process Coordinator/Designee Shift Leader Property Officer Physician or Licensed Psychologist Clinical Director Treatment Team Facilitator

A resident's right(s), as provided in K.S.A. 59-29a22(b)(15)-(22), may be denied or restricted: (1) for cause or (2) when medically or therapeutically contraindicated. For institutional management purposes or facility security, the denial or restriction of a resident's right(s), as provided in. KS.A. 59-29a22(b)(15)-(22), will begin as soon as the necessity for a denial or restriction arises. If the denial or restriction is modified or reversed, the resident's right will be restored within five working days of the reversal or modification.

All deadlines established in this policy may be extended for reasons of excusable delay or when additional time is needed to adequately and appropriately investigate the matter.

The resident and staff member should sign all relevant Notices, Requests, and the Record of Informal Hearing. If the resident refuses to sign any form mentioned in this policy, the staff member will note the resident's refusal to sign on the form. The resident's refusal to sign any Notices, Requests, or the Record of Informal Hearing does not preclude further review through this policy.

The Denial or Restriction of Resident Rights Form CPR-410's (A-E) will be referred to in this policy by; Form (A), Form (B), Form (C), Form (D), and Form (E). Blank copies of Form (A) and (D) will be accessible on every unit.

At each step of the process, the resident will be provided a copy of all relevant Notices, Requests, and the Record of Informal Hearings.

Steps of the Process:

1. K.S.A. 59-29a22(c): A resident's right(s), as provided in K.S.A. 59-29a22(b)(15)-(22), may be restricted or denied: (1) for cause or (2) when medically or therapeutically contraindicated.

2. For Cause Restrictions:

• If an SPTP staff member or Property Officer believes cause exists to deny or restrict a resident's right(s), as provided under K.S.A. 59-29a22(b) (15)-(22), the staff member must complete Form (B), describing:

(1) The right denied or restricted,

(2) The cause for the denial or restriction, and

(3) The rationale for the denial or restriction.

• The SPTP staff member or Property Officer must sign Form (B).

• The SPTP staff member or Property Officer will present Form (B) to the resident. The resident must sign, acknowledging receipt of Form (B). If the resident refuses to sign, the SPTP staff member or Property Officer will document the refusal to sign on the form.

• The SPTP staff member or Property Officer will make a copy of Form (B).

• The SPTP staff member or property Officer will provide the resident with a copy of signed Form (B).

• The SPTP staff member or Property Officer will deliver signed Form (B) to the SPTP Due Process Coordinator/Designee.

• The SPTP Due Process Coordinator will assign Form (B) a case number.

• The SPTP Due Process Coordinator/Designee will scan and upload signed Form (B) into the resident's medical record.

• The resident has three (3) working days to submit Form (D) to the SPTP Due Process Coordinator/Designee, along with a copy of the signed Form (B). After submission, the resident will be provided with a copy of the completed Form (D).

• The SPTP Due Process Coordinator/Designee will scan and upload signed Form (D) into the resident's medical record.

3. Medically or Therapeutically Contraindicated Restrictions:

• The resident's Physician, Licensed Psychologist, or Masters Level Psychologist completes Form (C), describing:

(1) The right denied or restricted,

(2) The length of time the right will be denied or restricted, and

(3) The reason why the exercise of the right is medically or therapeutically contraindicated.

• The resident's Physician, Licensed Psychologist, or Masters Level Psychologist must sign Form (C) and submit the form to the SPTP Due Process Coordinator/Designee.

• The SPTP Due Process Coordinator/Designee will present Form (C) to the resident.

• The resident must sign, acknowledging receipt of Form (C). If the resident refuses to sign, the SPTP Due Process Coordinator/Designee will document the refusal to sign on the form.

• The SPTP Due Process Coordinator/Designee will make a copy of signed Form (C).

• The SPTP Due Process Coordinator/Designee will provide the resident with a copy of Form (C).

• The SPTP Due Process Coordinator/Designee will scan and upload signed Form (C) into the resident's medical record.

• The resident has three days to submit Form (D) to the SPTP Due Process Coordinator/Designee, along with a copy of signed Form (C). After submission, the resident will be provided with a copy of the completed Form (D).

• The SPTP Due Process Coordinator/Designee will scan and upload signed Form (D) into the resident's medical record.

4. Resident Initiated Review of Denial or Restriction:

• If a resident believes a right, as provided in K.S.A. 59-29a22(b)(15)-(22), has been denied or restricted, and the resident has not received Form (B) or Form (C), the resident may complete Form (A), describing:

(1) The allegedly denied or restricted right, and

(2) A description of how the right has allegedly been denied or restricted.

• The resident has seven days from the date of the alleged denial or restriction to complete Form (A).

• The resident will give Form (A) to the SPTP Due Process Coordinator/Designee.

• Both the resident and SPTP Due Process Coordinator/Designee will sign Form (A).

• The SPTP Due Process Coordinator/Designee will provide a copy of signed Form (A) to the resident.

• The SPTP Due Process Coordinator/Designee will give Form (A) to the Clinical Director/ Designee within three days of receipt.

• The Clinical Director/Designee will conduct a review of the alleged denial or restriction to determine whether the alleged denial or restriction occurred.

• The Clinical Director/Designee will complete the Clinical Director's portion of Form (A) and return it to the SPTP Due Process Coordinator/Designee.

• The SPTP Due Process Coordinator/Designee will present the completed Form (A) to the resident. The SPTP Due Process Coordinator/Designee and the resident must sign, acknowledging receipt, of the completed Form (A). If the resident refuses to sign Form (A), the SPTP Due Process Coordinator/Designee will document the refusal to sign the Form.

• The SPTP Due Process Coordinator/Designee will make a copy of the completed Form (A).

• The SPTP Due Process Coordinator/Designee will provide the resident with a copy of Form (A).

• The SPTP Due Process Coordinator/Designee will scan and upload the completed Form (A) into the resident's medical record.

• If the Clinical Director/Designee determined the right has been denied, the resident has three days to submit Form (D) to the SPTP Due Process Coordinator/Designee, along with a copy of signed Form (A). After submission, the resident will be provided with a copy of the completed Form (D).

• The SPTP Due Process Coordinator/Designee will scan and upload signed Form (D) into the resident's medical record.

5. Informal Hearing Review:

• The informal hearing will be conducted by a Treatment Team Facilitator from a different LSH unit or program, or another person designated by the Superintendent and will be referred to as the Hearing Officer.

• The Hearing Officer will preside over the hearing, listen to the resident, and review the decisions of the Clinical Director, SPTP Staff member or Property Officer, or the resident's Physician, Licensed Psychologist or Masters Level Psychologist.

• After reviewing the written submissions of the resident and after hearing any statements or arguments made by the resident, the Hearing Officer will complete Form (E).

• The Hearing Officer will sign Form (E) and return it to the SPTP Due Process Coordinator/Designee.

• The SPTP Due Process Coordinator/Designee will present the completed Form (E) to the resident. The SPTP Due Process Coordinator/Designee and the resident must sign, acknowledging receipt of the completed Form (E). If the resident refuses to sign Form (E), the SPTP Due Process Coordinator/Designee will document the refusal to sign the form.

• The SPTP Due Process Coordinator/Designee will make a copy of the completed Form (E).

• The SPTP Due Process Coordinator/Designee will provide the resident with a copy of Form (E).

• The SPTP Due Process Coordinator/Designee will scan and upload the completed, signed Form (E) into the resident's medical record.

CHAPTER 6

VISITATION

—⋙∘⟨⟩∘⋘—

The next policy is the internal rules and process for visitation. The facility titles it as Policy 10.18 Resident Visitation. In bringing this one I have left off the title bar, procedure section, reference section, signature bar, and previous version dates.

POLICY
SPTP permits resident visitation under conditions that protect the resident, staff, and public; honor resident confidentiality; and preserve the need for a therapeutic environment.

Visitation will be available in areas away from the general population. Visitors will be required to produce photo identification (ID) to Safety/Security officers for review and verification upon arrival at the facility. Residents who are in seclusion, restraint, or Individual Person Management Plan administrative confinement at the time of the visit will not be allowed visitation unless approved by the Program Director/Designee.

Visitors under the age of 18 require prior approval by the Program Director/Designee in consultation with the Treatment team. See Child/Adolescent Specific Visitation Guidelines below.

Visits are subject to being denied or restricted by Program Director/Designee and/or Treatment Team pursuant to SPTP Policy No.: 8.6 - Denial or Restriction of Resident Rights. Visits are subject to being revoked, canceled, and/or terminated at the discretion of SPTP/LSH supervisory staff [CTS/Shift Leader, RN, Senior Ranking Officer (SRO), etc.].

A visitation request may be denied for the following reasons:

▪ The visitor has provided false information on the application(s) for visitation.

▪ The visitor has submitted incomplete information on the application(s) for visitation.

▪ There are reasonable grounds to believe the visitor's presence at the SPTP may pose a risk to the safety and security of the residents and/or staff.

▪ The Treatment Team has reasonable grounds to believe the resident's treatment progress would be significantly jeopardized by this visit.

▪ The visitor is a victim of the resident's past criminal activity.

▪ The visitor is currently under supervision by any criminal justice agency.

▪ The visitor is a registered sex offender.

▪ The visitor has current criminal charges.

▪ The visitor is a former employee of Larned State Hospital (LSH).

▪ The visitor has had prior criminal involvement with the resident.

▪ The visitor has a history of attempting to bring contraband, absolute contraband, and/or prohibited items into a secure facility. Refer to LSH Administrative policy, SE-10.0 Contraband and Allowable items.

▪ The visitor is a felon.

▪ The visitor has been denied visiting privileges in the past at the SPTP or any Department of Corrections (DOC) facility.

▪ There is no signed and dated approval of the parent or guardian of a proposed minor visitor.

NOTE: Residents who have left the program for a minimum of one year due to being returned to a DOC facility will be required to re-submit visitation applications upon return to the SPTP.

Visitors are required to present current ID upon arrival to the SPTP and prior to their visit. Acceptable forms of ID include the following

(one of the below is required):
- Valid State Driver's License
- Valid Military ID
- Department of Transportation (DOT) ID Card
- State issued Picture ID
- Passport (current)
- Birth certificate (child/adolescent only)

Multiple residents may have the same visitor(s) on their approved visitation list; however, the visitor may only visit one identified resident during any one visitation period. There may be exceptions to this requirement made by the Program Director/Designee under certain circumstances. All visitors must remain with the resident they are visiting and avoid other resident/visitor contact. Additionally, visitors should remain outside of non-visitation areas where other residents may be present.

No more than six approved visitors may visit during any one visitation period unless approved by the Program Director/Designee. If the number of persons reaches visitation area capacity, no further visitations will be allowed until space is available.

Visitation will occur on weekends and official state holidays. Unless otherwise notified, the visitation area for those residents residing on Dillon and Dillon Annex will be in Dillon Mod A; the visitation area for those residents residing on Jung is located at the front (East) entrance of Jung building, adjacent to the Jung Control Center; the visitation area for those residents residing on Isaac Ray is the Isaac Ray visitation area (corridor 113). Visiting hours are as follows:

Dillon, Dillon Annex, and Jung: 8:30 a.m. to 3:30 p.m.

Isaac Ray: 9:00 a.m. to 1:00 p.m.

If a visitor leaves the visitation area, for any purpose, they must again clear the security checkpoint prior to re-entry.

NOTE: There will be no access to the kitchen area or restrooms in Dillon Mod A and it will remain locked throughout visitation.

Special Visits may be approved through the Program Director/Designee [via the Sexual Predator Treatment Program, Resident Request Form (SPTP-30)]. Special Visits are visitations scheduled outside of the normal visitation days and may be approved when the visitor has traveled at least 200 miles, when it is anticipated that the number of visitors will exceed the approved limit, when the visitor is the resident's personal attorney, and/or other special circumstances.

NOTE: The LSH Chaplain will review the standing of all clergy within their denomination or affiliation before they are approved to visit any resident. Refer to LSH Patient policy, P9-03 Vetting Clergy and Church Professionals for Visitation.

It is not permissible to bring in or send out any property items (consumable or non-consumable) for residents through visitation unless approved by the Program Director/Designee. A reasonable amount of clothing may be pre-approved by utilizing the Resident Request Form (SPTP-30).

Unless approved in advance, visitors may only bring the following items into the visitation area:

- Coins (not to exceed $20 per adult visitor). No paper money is allowed in the visitation area. No exchange of money is permitted between residents and visitors. NOTE: Coins are not permitted for visitors of residents residing on the Isaac Ray building.
- 3" x 5" coin purse. NOTE: A coin purse is not permitted for visitors of residents residing on the Isaac Ray building.
- Emergency medications
- A reasonable amount of child care items

Lockers are available for storage of purses and other items not allowed in the visitation area. Items allowed within the visitation area must clear the tomography machine.

Dress Code for Visitors: The following apparel is considered inappropriate and will result in the denial of a visit. This dress code applies equally to men, women, and children.

- Transparent clothing
- Shorts which shorter than approximately two inches above the knee-cap
- Skirts or dresses shorter than approximately one inch above the kneecap
- Strapless, tube, or halter tops
- Tops which expose the midriff
- Tops which expose excessive cleavage
- Spandex, Lycra, athletic pants (skin tight), tights, or leotards
- Underwear worn as outer garments or over the top of other clothing
- Clothing with revealing holes or tears above fingertip length or above kneecap
- Clothing or accessories with obscene or profane writing, images, or

pictures
- Sunglasses (not allowed to be worn in visitation area)
- Gang or club-related clothing or insignia. This includes, but is not limited to, motorcycle jackets bearing club logos, etc.
- Clothing with excess metal beads, snaps, zippers, etc., should be avoided.
- Underwire bras should be avoided.
- All visitors must wear close-toed shoes for the entire visit.

General Guidelines for Residents During Visitation:
- Residents are expected to comply with all staff directives during visits.
- Residents are allowed to visit only with their own visitors.
- Residents must remain within the visitation area at all times.
- It is the resident's responsibility to inform his prospective visitors of his daily schedule, including treatment group times and other scheduled activities.
- Residents are not to handle money.
- Residents and visitors are not allowed to exchange property in the visitation area.

Physical contact is to be limited to embracing the visitor once at the beginning of the visit and again at the conclusion of the visit. "Embrace" equates to a brief hug. The visit will be terminated if physical contact is excessive. LSH Sexual Predator Treatment Program (SPTP) Policy & Procedure Manual – Policy #: 10.18 Effective: July 31_, 2016 Page 4 of 9

If contraband is found during a visit, staff shall seize and secure the contraband and end the visit. Staff shall then notify Safety/Security in the Dillon, Jung, or Isaac Ray Control Center(s), the appropriate Unit Leader, and the Program Director/Designee. Issues of contraband will lead to the visitor(s) being restricted from future visitation.

While on the grounds of LSH, all visitors must display appropriate behavior. Arguing, inappropriate language, name calling, yelling, threats, intimidation, verbal insults or other disruptive behavior will not be allowed. Additionally, visitors shall not display or engage in any sexual behavior/activity while on the grounds of LSH. If the behavior persists, Safety/Security will be contacted to assist in terminating the visit. Additionally, staff will contact the Unit Leader. The Unit Leader will then contact the Program Director/Designee. Inappropriate behavior will lead to the visit being terminated and the visitor(s) being restricted from future visitation.

Failure to comply with any of these guidelines will lead to a termination of the visit.

Child/Adolescent Specific Visitation Guidelines:

Child/Adolescent visitors are considered those under the age of eighteen years.

Appropriate behavior by the residents and their visitors is expected. Children/Adolescents are the responsibility of their parent/supervising adult. Staff will intervene if any inappropriate or abusive behavior by the resident and/or parent/supervising adult occurs towards the child and the visit will be terminated. Such behavior will be reported via an Incident Report (LSH-412).

Visitors under the age of eighteen require prior approval by the Program Director/Designee in consultation with the Treatment Team so as to avoid therapeutic contraindication. Arrangements for such a visit must be in place prior to the date of the actual visit. Children under six years of age shall be admitted as visitors only when approved by the Program Director/Designee in consultation with the Treatment Team so as to avoid therapeutic contraindication.

The Application for Visiting Privileges (Child / Adolescent Visitation) - SPTP (CPR-309B) must be completed at least thirty days prior to the initial visit and given to the Program Director/Designee along with the rest of the application packet. If multiple visitations are being requested for a particular visitation day, a first come/first serve system will be used. Child/Adolescent visits are subject to being denied, revoked, cancelled, and/or terminated at the discretion of the Program Director/Designee. A certified copy of the Child/Adolescent visitor's birth certificate must be included in the application unless the visitor has another acceptable form of ID as listed above. The certified copy of the birth certificate or other acceptable ID must also be presented to Safety/Security in the Dillon, Jung, or Isaac Ray Control Center(s) prior to each visit as this is the accepted form of identification for Child/Adolescent visitors. For subsequent visits, at least a five day notice is required prior to each visit as listed in the SPTP Resident Handbook.

It is the resident's and visitor's responsibility to provide sufficient information to the Program Director/Designee regarding the following: Relationship to resident, previous victimization of the Child/Adolescent by the resident, and written permission from the primary caregiver for the visit. This information must be contained in the application for visitation.

Once the initial approval for the Child/Adolescent visitation has been obtained, subsequent approval from the Treatment and Program Director/Designee is necessary for future visitations. LSH Sexual Predator Treatment Program (SPTP) Policy & Procedure Manual – Policy #: 10.18 Effective: July 31_, 2016 Page 5 of 9

Child/Adolescent visitations are only allowed on the second Saturday of the month and will be subject to the same visitation time frames listed above. Only Child/Adolescent visitation is allowed on this designated day. Child/Adolescent visitation will be allowed on Father's Day with approval and will occur in place of the Saturday designated for Child/Adolescent visitation in the month of June. No more than three Children/Adolescents may visit a resident during one visitation session.

A parent/supervising adult that has also been approved for visitation must accompany all Child/Adolescent visitors and be present during the visitation session.

All visitations are to be supervised by staff at all times, and the visits may be terminated by supervisory staff for any safety/security reason or any violation of the LSH and/or SPTP policies or guidelines governing visitation. If visitation is terminated, staff shall follow SPTP Policy No.: 8.6 Denial or Restriction of a Resident Right.

SPTP Resident Guidelines to Request Visitation:

A. The resident must indicate on the Authorization for Disclosure of Information (MS-200G1) the prospective visitor's information (as indicated on the form). The resident must sign the form. If a resident does not sign the form the visitation will not occur.

B. The resident must request and receive approval for all first time visitors:

1. Resident will request an Application for Visiting Privileges - SPTP (CPR-309A) from unit staff.

2. Resident will mail the prospective visitor an Application for Visiting Privileges - SPTP (CPR-309A). One application for each visitor is required. The prospective visitor must complete the form and mail it back to the SPTP. The application will be reviewed and a determination will be made as to whether or not the requested visitor will be approved for visitation. This must occur before any first time visit can take place.

3. For first time Child/Adolescent visitation, the Application for Vis-

iting Privileges (Child / Adolescent Visitation) - SPTP (CPR-309B) must be completed at least thirty days prior to the initial visit and given to the Program Director/Designee along with an Application for Visiting Privileges - SPTP (CPR-309A) for the Child/Adolescent and parent/ supervising adult.

C. Each time a resident wants to visit with an approved visitor, he must submit a Request for Visitation - SPTP (CPR-34) at least five (5) days prior to the visit: Resident will complete the Request for Visitation - SPTP (CPR-34) and turn it into a unit staff member. NOTE: The resident will receive a copy of the completed Request for Visitation - SPTP (CPR-34).

D. The resident will submit to a full frisk search and being searched via a handheld metal detector before proceeding to and at the completion of the visit.

E. The resident is not permitted to take any items to the visitation area; however, it is permissible for the resident's Primary Treatment Facilitator to leave specific paperwork items with Safety/Security in the Dillon, Jung, or Isaac Ray Control Center(s) (in a sealed manila envelope, marked with the resident's name) which the resident can show to his visitor(s). Only documents that fit within one standard size manila envelope will be permitted (Comprehensive Integrated Treatment Plan (CITP), relapse prevention plan, drawings, etc.). Any paperwork left with Safety/Security in the Dillon, Jung, or Isaac Ray Control Center(s) by the Primary Treatment Facilitator must be returned to Safety/Security in the Dillon, Jung, or Isaac Ray Control Center(s) at the conclusion of the visit. These items will then be returned to the resident's Primary Treatment Facilitator by Safety/Security during normal business hours.

F. For any Special Visits, the resident must submit a Sexual Predator Treatment Program, Resident Request Form (SPTP-30) through the Program Director/Designee.

Special Rules for Telecommunication (Skype) Visitation:

A. The Program Director/Designee may approve special telecommunication visits if requested by residents. This decision will be based on factors such as distance from the facility, health of the visitor, security status of the resident, facility management, etc.

B. Resident telecommunication visits are limited to one request per quarter unless approved for an extenuating circumstance by the Program Director/Designee.

C. The visitor camera shall only show the visitor from the shoulders up.

D. Only approved visitor(s) shall be in view during the visit or the visit will be stopped.

E. There shall be nothing of note within the background of the visitor camera.

F. Staff will be required to watch the visitor during the entire visit.

G. Visits via telecommunication (Skype) will last no more than one hour per visiting session.

H. The visitor or visitors must provide photo ID to the supervising staff member prior to the resident viewing the visitor.

I. Telecommunication (Skype) visits will occur only in the Dillon Medical Conference Room, the Jung North Conference Room, or the Isaac Ray N2 Conference Room.

J. All other visitation rules apply.

CHAPTER 7

CONTRABAND

————————————

The next policy is the policy drafted to comply with the requirements set forth in K.S.A. § 21-5914. The facility titles it as Policy 10.0 Contraband. In bringing this one I have left off the title bar, reference section, signature bar, and previous version dates.

PURPOSE
To clarify what items are considered contraband in the Sexual Predator Treatment Program (SPTP) at Larned State Hospital.

POLICY
I. Contraband Overview Residents may not cause contraband to be in the SPTP or be in possession of contraband while in the SPTP.

A. Contraband In General Generally, contraband includes, but is not limited to:

1. Any item, part of an item, or instructions on the creation of an

item, that is inherently capable of causing damage or injury to persons or property, may assist in an escape, or is capable or likely to produce or precipitate dangerous situations or conflict and that is not specifically authorized or permitted by LSH.

2. Any item that can be the basis for a charge of felony and/or misdemeanor for its possession under the laws of Kansas or the United States.

3. Any item that, although authorized, is misused or modified and if the item in its misused or modified form has the capability of being able to cause damage or injury to persons or property or likely to precipitate dangerous situations or conflicts.

4. Any item that would constitute a violation of K.S.A. 21-5914 "Traffic in contraband in a correctional institution or care and treatment facility."

5. Unless authorized by SPTP, any item prohibited pursuant to LSH or SPTP rules.

6. All contraband shall be confiscated and shall be forfeited by the resident.

7. No resident shall possess, hold, sell, transfer, receive, control, or distribute any contraband.

B. Tobacco Contraband

1. No resident shall possess, hold, sell, transfer, receive, control, or distribute tobacco products, tobacco substitutes, or smoking paraphernalia, except for as specified in subsection C of this paragraph.

2. For the purposes of this regulation, each of the following terms shall have the meaning specified in this subsection:

a. "Tobacco products" means cigarettes, cigars, pipe tobacco, looseleaf tobacco, chewing tobacco, and smokeless tobacco. This term shall not include pharmacological aids for smoking cessation approved by the food and drug administration.

b. "Tobacco substitutes" means any substance ingested by smoking, and/or any herbal or leaf-based replacements for chewing tobacco. This term shall not include any controlled substance.

c. "Smoking paraphernalia" means pipes, lighters, matches, altered batteries, cigarette papers, rolling machines, and all other items fabricated, developed, or processed for the primary purpose of facilitating the use or possession of tobacco products or tobacco substitutes.

3. Residents may engage in bona fide religious activities sanctioned

by the program involving the use and possession of tobacco products, tobacco substitutes, and smoking paraphernalia as permitted by and in accordance with the LSH/SPTP policies and procedures for use in an approved religious activity.

C. Stimulants, Sedatives, Drugs, or Narcotics

1. No resident shall ingest, inhale, inject, or introduce by any other means any kind of substance into the resident's body or the body of another resident that is capable of producing intoxication, hallucinations, stimulation, depression, dizziness, or any other alteration of the resident's state of consciousness or feeling, except for the following:

a. Approved foods and beverages. Alcohol in any form shall not be deemed an approved food or beverage unless the alcohol is a medicinal ingredient in an authorized or prescribed medication.

b. Any legal drugs, including medication properly and legally prescribed or authorized for the resident by an authorized, licensed physician.

2. The misuse or hoarding, as defined below, of any authorized or prescribed medication is not permitted:

a. Misuse shall mean any use other than that for which the medication was specifically authorized or prescribed.

b. Hoarding shall mean having possession or control of, or holding any quantity of authorized or prescribed medication greater than the amount or dosage that has been issued to the resident by medical staff, or greater than the amount that should be remaining if the resident has taken the medication in accordance with the prescription and instructions from medical staff.

3. Residents, while in possession or control of medication, shall not leave the medical unit or area where the medication is issued, unless the removal of the medication from the unit or area has been authorized in writing by medical staff.

II. Examples of Contraband

Contraband includes but may not be limited to:

A. Weapons

1. Pocket or hunting knives.

2. Weapons such as firearms, knives, explosives, or like items, including items crafted or created for the purpose of causing bodily harm or destruction of property.

3. Ammunition.

4. Explosives or explosive-making materials.

B. Alcohol and Drugs

1. Alcohol, "hooch", or illicit substances.

2. Alcohol based items unless preapproved in writing.

3. Paraphernalia or anything depicting alcoholic beverages

4. Any unapproved prescription or over the counter medications including by not limited to ibuprofen, medicated creams, and Sudafed.

5. Illegal drugs, drug paraphernalia, items depicting drugs or drug use, or designer drugs including but not limited to K2 and bath salts.

6. Tobacco contraband as detailed above.

7. Medical items including but not limited to knee braces, bandages, and gauze that do not have current physician orders.

8. Any other stimulants, sedative, drug, or narcotic.

C. Tools

1. Wire cutters and/or bolt cutters.

2. Tools including but not limited to dremel, soldering gun, battery testers/volt meters, wood burning, wrenches, and screwdrivers.

3. Personal tools excluding approved craft items.

4. Metal utensils including but not limited to knives, forks, and spoons.

5. Nails, nuts/bolts, screws, and other similar items excluding approved craft items.

6. Tattoo guns whether purchased or homemade and ink or other products intended to be used for creating tattoos.

7. Loose pieces of wood.

8. Tape of any kind. Residents may ask and receive clear tape pieces, not to exceed any piece over 3 inches in length. NOTE: Items approved, in writing, for craft projects will be allowed.

D. Media, Devices, or Accessories

1. Sexual products or sexual appliances.

2. Flashlights or a similar device.

3. Personal kitchen appliances including, but not limited to: refrigerators, electric skillets, crock pots, microwaves, toasters, and popcorn poppers unless these items have been approved, in writing.

4. Devices and media deemed contraband under SPTP Policy No.: 5.18 Resident Media.

5. Catalog where the primary focus is children or there are children on numerous pages.

6. Items identified in SPTP Policy No.: 8.3 -Resident Mail as unap-

proved.

E. Miscellaneous

1. Metal containers.

2. Glass or any item containing glass, including consumable items. The only permitted items containing glass include but may not be limited to prescription eye glasses and/or approved reading glasses and limited approved light bulbs.

3. Currency or money including but not limited to cash, change, and money orders.

4. Cardboard boxes or storage containers that are not approved such as milk crates.

5. Personal or state property that has been altered from its original form or original and intended function.

6. Other items deemed to be a danger to staff or residents.

7. Flammable or toxic substances and any item labeled flammable or toxic.

8. Items taken from an Activity Therapy area without authorization.

9. Plastic bags of any kind, with the exception of quart-sized "zip lock" bags.

10. Aerosol cans including but not limited to air fresheners, deodorant, shaving cream, hairspray, and cheese wiz.

11. Canned food items.

12. Stuffed animals, novelty pillows, throw pillows, or any stuffed item smaller than a standard sized pillow.\

13. Candles or wax melting devices.

14. Items determined by the Clinical Team or Treatment Team to be related to a resident's pattern of offending or other criminal behavior.

15. Glass and metal, including but not limited to clothing ornaments such as conchos, dog tags, containers with metal lids, and any other item deemed by the Program Director to be a danger to the safety and security of the residents, public, staff, unit, or facility. '

16. Property of another.

17. Leather or suede material.

18. Items deemed to endanger the safety and security of the unit, facility, public, resident, or staff, including but not limited to, state or local maps, or maps that may be contraindicated to a resident's treatment.

III. Items Allowed with Approval

Certain items listed within this policy may be allowed with the proper authorization using CPR-399 Property Variance form.

IV. Consequences of Policy Violations A violation of one or more rules within this policy that does not have a specific consequence noted could result in a notification report and subsequent consequence to include any or all of the following:

A. Restriction status, not to exceed (90) days

B. Restriction from purchasing, not to exceed (90) days

C. Reduction in privilege level

D. Forfeiture of contraband. NOTE: Contraband seized will be disposed of after 90 days, or if applicable, upon completion of the appeals process.

CHAPTER 8

PATIENT FOOD

⸻◈◦◖◗◦◈⸻

T he next policy is the policy drafted to set the rules for food. The facility titles it as Policy P5-08 Patient Food Storage and Preparation Expectations. In bringing this one I have left off the title bar, reference section, signature bar, and previous version dates.

PURPOSE
The purpose of this policy is to identify limitations and expectations regarding food and food management in Larned State Hospital patient rooms and units.
POLICY
Larned State Hospital is to ensure the following limitations and expectations are followed by all patients.
A. Bulk foods, perishable foods, or opened containers of food are not to be stored in patient rooms. A reasonable supply (approximately one

week supply) of unopened, individual serving products may be stored in patient rooms.

B. Partially eaten foods or prepared food products are not to be kept in patient rooms.

C. Food products are not to be stored on the floor in patient rooms, unit kitchens, pantries, or any other areas.

D. No cooking of any kind is allowed in patient rooms. Coffee makers, if allowed in patient rooms, must be kept clean and used for the sole purpose of making coffee. (NOTE: Not all programs or units allow coffee makers in individual rooms.)

E. No meals shall be prepared in unit kitchens.

F. Select single-serve, microwaveable products may be allowed and may be heated in microwave ovens. Such items must be consumed only by the individual who owns the product. (NOTE: Use of hair nets and gloves is not needed in these circumstances as the patient heating the product is the only person consuming the product.) Frozen or refrigerated microwaveable products are only allowed as per individual program policy.

G. On Psychiatric Services Program any "Family Gifts" of food products must be stored and consumed according to LSH Patient Policy and Procedure P2-15, "Refrigerator/Freezer and Dry Storage in Patient Areas." Such food products are to be consumed only by the person who owns the product.

H. All refrigerated or otherwise perishable products labeled and stored according to LSH Patient Policy P2-15, "Refrigerator/Freezer and Dry Storage in Patient Areas. Patients and Tier Two Residents are allowed to purchase perishable products as part of their treatment at LSH only as described in individual program policies.

NOTE: Patients must assume responsibility for ensuring their food storage, food preparation, and food consumption activities meet the cleanliness expectations of the individual units. The hospital reserves the right to restrict such practices, on a case-by-case or unit-by-unit basis, for a limited or extended period of time, if sufficient clinical or administrative determination warrants such action.

CHAPTER 9

SEARCHES

--------------◇○◖◗○◇--------------

The next policy is the policy drafted to set the rules for searches. The facility titles it as Policy P9-11 Searching Patient's/Resident's Possessions. In bringing this one I have left off the title bar, reference section, signature bar, and previous version dates.

PURPOSE

To provide for a safe and secure environment, this policy defines the conditions when a patient's/resident's possessions may be searched.

POLICY

The Administrative and Clinical Program Director, Assistant Director of Nursing, Unit Leader, or Shift Leader may implement a search of a patient's/resident's possessions. Searches may be conducted for reasonable cause, or routine reasons, to include but not be limited to:

1. To ensure the safety of the patient/resident(s) or others and maintain an effective therapeutic environment by locating absolute contra-

band, minimizing excessive or combustible items, or other prohibited property.

2. To ascertain whether a specific item, which belongs to another patient/resident, the State of Kansas, or a staff member, is among the patient's/resident's belongings (there must be reason to believe that the item might be found in the patient's/resident's possessions).

Staff will be respectful of patient's/resident's personal and religious items and take necessary precautions to minimally disrupt and not damage patient/resident property while conducting the search. If warranted, the LSH Chaplain/designee may be contacted to be present while religious items are searched. For the purpose of this policy, the designee for the Chaplain would be the Sexual Predator Treatment Program (SPTP) Administrative Program Director, SPTP Program Manager, or SPTP Program Leader. If the LSH Chaplain/designee is not available, the items the patient/resident is objecting to having searched will be sealed in an evidence bag and held by Security until the LSH Chaplain/designee can inspect the items. If questions arise, the Administrative Program Director/Designee should be consulted.

CHAPTER 10

MEDIA

The next policy is the policy drafted to set the rules for media. The facility titles it as Policy 5.18 Resident Media. In bringing this one I have left off the title bar, reference section, signature bar, and previous version dates.

PURPOSE

The purpose of this policy is to regulate the possession of media by the residents of the Sexual Predator Treatment Program (SPTP). These rules are established to prevent the introduction of sexually explicit material, media that is counter therapeutic to treatment, or other contraband into the facility.

POLICY

I. Media Defined

For the purposes of this policy, media is defined as any book, magazine, drawing, painting, writing, picture, movie, video game, item, device, or any similar object containing a visual, verbal, or auditory depiction, or theme.

II. Media Deemed Contraband

The following media is considered contraband in the SPTP and is prohibited:

A. Sexual Explicit Material shall be considered sexually explicit if:

1. The purpose of the material is for sexual arousal or gratification;

2. Contains nudity, which shall be defined as the depiction or display of any state of undress in which the (1) human genitals, (2) pubic region, (3) buttock, or (4) female breast at a point below the top of the areola, are less than completely and opaquely covered; or

3. Containing any display, actual or simulated, or description of any of the following: (1) sexual intercourse or sodomy, including genital-genital, oral genital, anal-genital, and anal-oral contact, whether between persons of the same or differing gender, (2) masturbation, (3) bestiality, (4) sado-masochistic abuse, or (5) the exploitation of any person under the age of 18 years.

B. Medically or Therapeutically Contraindicative

Material Media containing material and/or themes considered contraindicative to a resident's treatment by the primary treatment facilitator and/ or treatment team including, but not limited to, the following:

1. Media containing depictions of a race, age, gender, etc., associated with a SPTP resident's prior offending patterns.

2. Media containing depictions of torture in the form of bondage, dominance, submission, and sadomasochism.

3. Media containing material and/or themes that could compromise the safety and security of SPTP and/or the community, containing but not limited to themes of escaping from facilities.

4. Media containing graphic depictions of injury and/or death, extreme and/or realistic blood, gore, weapons, or scenes depicting bloodless dismemberment.

C. Other

Material For safety and security purposes, the following items are prohibited:

1. Media lacking an industry-standard rating

2. Video games rated "M" or higher

3. VHS Tapes

4. Rewritable media

5. Recording and picture-taking devices

6. Cellular telephones and cellular phone accessories such as chargers, SD cards, or other memory type cards

7. Electronic surveillance or monitoring devices, electronic transmitters, binoculars, cameras or voice, audio, video recorders

8. PDAs, or any related communication device, or any accessories

9. Electronic devices with wireless or LAN internet connections/capacity to connect to the internet

10. Extension cords

11. SD cards and/or other media storage devices such as USB flash drives excluding floppy disks for computers

12. Personal computers, laptops, or other computer accessories/components

13. Local newspapers and phonebooks

CHAPTER 11

TREATMENT

—————————⊸०⌒⌒०⊸—————————

The next policy is the policy drafted to set the rules for treatment. The facility titles it as Policy 6.1 Treatment. In bringing this one I have left off the title bar, reference section, signature bar, and previous version dates.

PURPOSE
The purpose of this policy is to explain the treatment model used in the Sexual Predator Treatment Program (SPTP) at Larned State Hospital (LSH).

POLICY
SPTP provides individualized therapeutic treatment to all residents. This policy explains the treatment models used in the program, the process for the admission and assessment of residents, for the evaluation of a resident's progress within the treatment tiers, and for making decisions to assign a resident to a high, medium, or low risk group as well as pro-

vide supplemental therapy groups based on the Risk Needs Responsivity Model.

PROCEDURE

I. Overview

Upon admission into the SPTP, residents will be placed on the Assessment and Orientation Tier which will evaluate and assess residents to determine residents' individualized risk and treatment needs. Once the Assessment and Orientation Tier ha& been completed, residents may move to Tier One to focus on skill acquisition which provides residents the tools to effectively identify their individual risk and courses to decrease re-offense. Once skills have been acquired and Tier One has been completed, and residents are approved by the Progress Review Panel (PRP), residents may move to Tier Two for skill demonstration which provides residents with the tools to move from highly structured inpatient treatment toward an independent lifestyle. Once Tier Two has been completed, and residents are approved by the PRP, residents may move to Tier Three where they will be placed in a Reintegration Facility and demonstrate their ability to translate the principles of offense-free behavior they learned at LSH to a real world environment.

Once ready, residents may petition the original committing Court for Transitional Release where they will continue therapy and reside at one of the reintegration facilities, while looking for long-term housing and complete an approved Conditional Release Plan. Following the successful completion of the reintegration process, SPTP may recommend residents to the Court for movement into Conditional Release. If the Court approves, residents will be discharged from SPTP and live in the community, under the supervision of the Court.

II. Treatment

A. Orientation and Assessment Tier

1. All new admissions will be placed into the Assessment and Orientation Tier during which an extensive evaluation and assessment will take place to determine individual risks, treatment needs, intellectual abilities, and supplemental groups. A Comprehensive Individualized Treatment Plan (CITP) will be developed.

2. Assessments and evaluation will be individualized based on residents' intellectual abilities and mental health needs in addition to the Static-99R and Sex Offender Treatment Intervention and Progress Scale

(SOTIPS).

3. Residents will also begin the treatment process in weekly groups where residents will complete an autobiography and victim sheets.

B. Tier One -Skill Acquisition

1. Tier Goal: The goal of Tier One is to provide residents with skill acquisition by attending therapy, courses, and supplemental groups while also focusing on their individual risks and needs.

2. Resident Track: Once the Orientation and Assessment Tier has been completed, the treatment team will determine whether residents will move forward in either the Mainstream Track or the Parallel Track.

a. The Parallel Track is used for residents with intellectual developmental disabilities or other disabilities that would hinder their ability to succeed in the mainstream track. It covers the same content as the mainstream program of SPTP but presents the material in a format which is more concrete and repetitive in order to facilitate learning.

b. Residents are given the opportunity to practice the concepts by using role-playing exercises. Additional help and study sessions are offered as needed.

3. Therapy Overview: The amount and type of therapy a resident will receive will be individualized to each resident's needs and risk. Within the Mainstream and Parallel Track, based on the Risk Needs Responsivity (RNR) model and initial assessments, residents will be placed in High (three hours per week), Medium (two hours per week) or Low Risk (one hour per week) therapy groups, a Relapse Prevention group, Cognitive Behavioral Therapy (CBT) for Sexual Offenders group, Basic CBT groups and Power of Emotion group.

4 Supplemental Groups: The treatment team can assign residents to additional manualized evidenced based groups based on their individual needs and risks. These groups can include but are not limited to CBT for Trauma, CBT for Depression and Anxiety, Interpersonal Psychological Therapy (IPT) for Psychosis, Living with a Personality Disorder, Power of Attitude, Boundaries and Relationships, Anger Management, Empathy and Substance Use and Aftercare.

C. Tier Two -Skill Demonstration

1. Tier Goal: The goal of this tier is to begin the process of moving from a highly structured inpatient program of treatment toward an essentially independent lifestyle. The resident will begin to start the process of moving away from a mind-set of institutionalization to growing self-de-

termination. Tier Two includes re-introduction and acclimatization to the real world through a graduated series of escorted outings -meals, shopping, recreation and the demonstration by the resident of the ability to make appropriate decisions about the use of one's own time.

2. Treatment Overview: Residents assigned to Tier Two will participate in the Good Lives Model and Self-Regulation group as well as a therapy group to discuss high risk factors, sexual thoughts and update their relapse prevention plans based on experiences during the supervised outings into the community.

3. Courses: Residents will also participate in classes designed to assist and prepare them for community reintegration to include but not limited to Healthy Transitional Living, Moral Decisions, Community Reintegration and Health Education. These classes are designed to help familiarize residents with using computers, cell phones, online job applications and become comfortable with the technological advances of society while still making appropriate and safe decisions. In addition, residents will begin to learn how to manage their finances, protect their financial credit, care for their medical and health issues, complete resumes and participate in mock job interviews.

4. Polygraphs: Resident will complete polygraphs every six months following the same polygraph procedures described in Tier One. In some cases, a resident may be required to take an additional polygraph if the Treatment Team feels that it is warranted based on residents' individual treatment plan.

5. Reintegration: Reintegration begins on Tier Two and is designed to be a safe and gradual movement from an inpatient treatment experience to the environment of open society. During this process the resident will maintain the foundation for personal change they have established in the SPTP while acquiring the skills necessary to be a responsible, contributing, offense-free member of our society.

6. Supplemental Outings: While on Tier Two, residents will begin to demonstrate the skills taught in the program and practice their relapse prevention plan through multiple supervised community outings. See Tier Two Outing Handbook.

7. Progress to Tier Three: Residents on Tier Two may request advancement to Tier Three at one of the reintegration facilities. The request will be evaluated and decided on by PRP in connection with recommendations from the Treatment Team and review residents' progression

through the program.

D. Program Aspects

1. Penile Plethysmograph (PPG)

a. The PPG is used to measure a physiological response to visual and/ or auditory stimuli. PPG results provide information about deviant sexual arousal which should be used in conjunction with a variety of other assessment tools and clinical expertise.

b. Assessments utilizing the PPG may be warranted during the initial orientation and assessment of a resident. PPG assessments may occur on Tier One or Tier Two if recommended by the treatment team. In Tier One these assessments will identify overall sexual arousal patterns and assess treatment effects of any pharmacological or behavioral interventions employed. In Tier Two these assessments will continue to assess treatment effects of any pharmacological or behavioral interventions employed and identify any changes in sexual arousal patterns once the resident begins community outings.

2. Leisure Activity Therapy There are a variety of leisure opportunities available to the residents at SPTP. While many of these sessions are open sessions that do not require the resident to enroll in, several sessions are only available to residents who sign up for them at quarterly enrollment sessions due to location or nature of the session. While there is not a required level of attendance in leisure activity sessions, residents are encouraged to participate in a variety of leisure activities that will enhance their physical and mental health and encourage healthy interpersonal relationships and interactions with others. Please refer to Activity Therapy policies.

3. Vocational Training Program The Vocational Training Program (VTP) provides residents opportunities to increase their knowledge and skills to enhance their employability and move towards reintegration. Residents may apply for an open VTP position if they have reached and are maintaining the highest privilege level, participated in treatment, and demonstrated progress in their individualized treatment plan. See SPTP VTP Manual; SPTP Policy No.: 5.8 -Privilege Levels.

III. Tier Three -Community Reintegration

A. Tier Goal: Tier Three provides a safe way for residents to demonstrate their ability to translate the principles of offense-free behavior they have learned at LSH to a real world environment. Residents in Tier

Three will continue the progress made by on Tier Two of Reintegration with the next logical step: a new, more realistic environment with its own structure to which the resident must make a successful adjustment. Residents will learn and exhibit the skills necessary to handle typical societal responsibilities such as finding employment, managing income, paying bills and constructively structuring individual time.

B. Reintegration Facility: Tier Three takes place at one of the reintegration facilities currently housed on the grounds of Larned State Hospital (Meyer House East), Osawatomie State Hospital (MiCo), and Parsons State Hospital (Maple House and Willow House). These facilities are designed to offer residents on Tier Three of SPTP and Transitional Release a safe, step-by-step way of moving into an outpatient mode of functioning. These facilities allow residents to demonstrate their ability to manage the responsibilities of an independent, responsible lifestyle and to make good judgments in a variety of real world situations, while still operating under the support of SPTP supervision.

C. Treatment Overview: Residents on Tier Three continue to participate in therapy with a treatment provider that is contracted through KDADS. Residents are expected to gain employment, establish a viable means of transportation by either purchasing a mode of transportation or utilizing public transportation, demonstrate financial stability, and develop an approved support network. Residents are provided with a stipend to pay rent, purchase their food, and care for their personal needs. Residents' rent and stipend are based on a· sliding scale determined by their income. The end goal is to assist residents resident in becoming self-sufficient when they apply for Transitional Release. See SPTP Reintegration Facility Handbook.

D. Polygraphs and PPG: Resident will complete polygraphs every six months following the same polygraph procedures described in Tier One. In some cases, a resident may be required to take an additional polygraph if the Treatment Team feels that it is warranted based on residents' individual treatment plan. Additionally, residents are subject to PPG testing if recommended by their Treatment Team.

E. Progress to Transitional Release: Successful Tier Three residents are recommended to the Court for Transitional Release by the SPTP.

IV. Transitional Release

Once ready, residents are required to petition the original committing Court for Transitional Release and are only placed on Transitional Release through a court order. Transitional Release builds on the work residents have previously done and provides a clear demonstration of their readiness for a relatively independent and healthy lifestyle. While on Transitional Release, residents continue therapy and reside at one of the reintegration facilities, while they look for long-term housing and complete an approved Conditional Release Plan.

V. Conditional Release

Following the successful completion of the reintegration process, SPTP may recommend residents to the Court for movement into Conditional Release. Once ready, residents are required to petition the courts for Conditional Release and are only placed on Conditional Release through a court order.

If the Court approves, residents will be discharged from SPTP and live in the community, under the supervision of the Court, for a minimum of five years; the precise length of time is determined by the Court. SPTP loses supervisory responsibility of residents once granted Conditional Release by the Court.

APPENDIX A

I would like to propose a new beneficial class be allowed in SPTP. The class would be a two part course and allow residents to earn a College Degree or High School Diploma with no expense to the Program. The benefits of this far outweigh the reasons to deny said class.

This course is necessary in SPTP for some colleges require test proctors in order to complete the course. This provides a class whereby this can occur for the proctor provided by the facility is already scheduled to be in the class and available.

Benefits

As with any part of this program it is best if there is a benefit to what is being proposed to be started. College would be very beneficial to this program for the following reasons: (1) Something New; (2) Recidivism; (3) Self-Esteem and Sense of Accomplishment; and (4) Preparedness for Reintegration.

Something New

At the end of every quarter residents are informed of the classes for the next quarter. This is usually met with comments like "Why do I have to take something I have already taken several times?" "There is nothing new," etc. How do we solve this, or can it be solved?

This course proposal offers a solution to the problem. The course is split into two parts. The first quarter one would learn about college and their options. After this and completion of an education plan they would then be enrolled in the second part until they achieve their goal. To be described further later.

This allows them to set their own treatment and courses into action and not have to repeat so many courses. They would have no reason to be negative towards the repeat nature of the program. Each quarter they would have something new and fresh.

This could be the motivation to achieve greater success in the program.

Recidivism

The goal of the program is to lower recidivism rates for those confined and to treat the issue that causes them to be dangerous. In regards to College and receiving a degree, studies have been done to determine the effect it has on recidivism.

The University of Emory Department of Economics studied the effect an education has on recidivism rates, or likelihood to reoffend. They found: "an inmate that has at least some high school education recidivates at a rate of 55%. When the inmate adds some vocational training to his educational toolbox, the offender's recidivism rate falls to 20%, and the rate continues to fall with each additional level of education. Again--quoting from a secondary report--Zoukis acknowledges that the recidivism rate is dramatically reduced when prisoners are afforded the opportunity of participating in post-secondary education. An inmate who earns an associate's degree presents a recidivism rate of only 13.7%; earning a bachelor's degree reduces that rate to 5.6%; and an inmate who earns a master's degree presents a recidivism rate of 0%." Article: The Mind Oppressed: Recidivism As A Learned Behavior, 6 Wake Forest J. L. & Pol'y 357.

Allowing or providing an ability for resident's to take college courses would meet the goal of lowering recidivism rates.

Self-Esteem and Sense of Accomplishment

I hear all the time how resident's state they feel those of us doing college are better than them or that they just could not accomplish a college degree even if they wanted to. I respond with encouragement that it is not as difficult as they think, but they cannot grasp it.

This course would allow them to see that it can be achieved and that they are not as lacking as they believe. It also fosters a sense of achievement. I believe the therapy department could shed more light on this benefit. Suffice it to say the potential is great.

Preparedness for Reintegration

I had the privilege of being in Reintegration until I erred. What I learned is that the jobs available are hard and laborious. As the population gets older here it will be harder for the men to get a productive job due to the laborious nature without education.

I had education prior to going to Reintegration and it was of great benefit to me. It helped me earn a higher wage and be offered more job opportunities and possibilities.

In addition the main reason one is in reintegration for so long is comfort and lack of money. Most do not know how the world works today and it takes awhile to adapt this is resolved for many college courses teach basic life skills, for example taxes, banking, computer, etc. as to lack of money the laborious jobs for the uneducated do not pay very well and if a resident had an education they could earn more and possibly complete reintegration faster.

The education provides life skills and training for many areas faced in Reintegration.

Plan

The course would be a two part course. The first part would take one quarter to complete and would teach everything to the resident about what he needs to know to start an education. The second part would be a continual class every quarter.

The first class is broke down into twelve lessons. These are set as follows:

Lesson 1: Introduction
Lesson 2: What is College
Lesson 3: Accreditation
Lesson 4: Financing an Education
Lesson 5: High School
Lesson 6: Schools and Options
Lesson 7: What an Education Plan is
Lesson 8: Parts of an Education Plan
Lesson 9: Education Plan Creation
Lesson 10: Education Resume/Portfolio
Lesson 11: Education Resume/Portfolio Review
Lesson 12: Review

The second class would be held once or twice a week for an hour. In this class the residents would be working on their college course material. This also allows for residents to help others grasp and learn the material. It also provides a Test Proctor for the courses that need a test proctor.

The advancements of this class can be great and would be discussed in detail in the next few sections.

Growth Opportunities

The ability of this class to grow into something more is only limited by what the program will or will not allow. Some areas of growth are: (1) VTP; (2) Test taking; (3) More Course Opportunities; (4) Lower costs; (5) Student becomes the Teacher; and (6) Graduation Ceremonies.

VTP

The program currently offers jobs in the facility through the Vocational Training Program. This program could be expanded to reward one who earns a college degree, thereby giving further incentive to seek an education and provide real world work experience.

In the world one who has no education is always paid at a lower rate than one who has an education. This can be taught by adding it to the VTP Program. It could be structured as follows:

One with no education starts at $7.25 (Minimum Wage Per Hour) and is capped at $7.40 per hour.

One with an Associate's Degree or Diploma or Certificate starts at $7.45 per hour and is capped at $7.60 per hour.

One with a Bachelor's Degree starts at $7.65 per hour and is capped at $7.80 per hour.

One with a Master's Degree starts at $7.85 per hour and is capped at $8.00 per hour.

One with a Doctorate starts at $8.05 per hour and is capped at $8.60 per hour.

This would then allow a resident to equate their education to worth for real world job experience. It also shows that the value of an education is real. This can make the VTP program more beneficial.

Test Taking

When the class starts the resident's will need to submit their tests, homework and exams by mail. This is a slow process that has been streamlined by some schools today. The schools allow them to be submitted online, by fax, or by telephone in certain circumstances. The classroom where this class is held could include the equipment necessary for a resident to utilize these faster methods.

The growth potential is great and can be streamlined by making technology available. It also helps the person build computer or personal skills dependent on the method they use.

More Course Opportunities

Today most schools offer more courses and opportunities if the resident can access their website. The Department of Corrections does this and the classroom where this is held could have computers with this access. It would be fully monitored by the one overseeing the class. It can also have an agreement signed that any inappropriate behavior will be met with extreme consequences.

This provides the benefit of more access to colleges and also teaches necessary but vital computer skills to the resident before he goes to Reintegration.

Lower Costs

There are many ways to lower the costs for a resident wanting to take college courses. Most know the most expensive item is books, this can be reduced by:

Providing Interlibrary Loan for the residents to get their books;

Allow for the class to be in a room where residents can donate books, that only those in the class can use at class time to complete their credits, without needing to purchase them.

Previously presented was the cost savings by using the telephone and internet for submission over postal service. This can save a lot of money for the resident. In addition the VTP pay scale based on education would help one have funds to cover the costs.

Providing the necessary tax forms each year for the Education credit will help to offset the costs for the resident seeking their education.

Student Becomes the Teacher

If the facility wants to be forward thinking they can apply to be a CLEP/DANTES special testing center. This would allow the facility to administer exams in places of college courses for the residents to earn college courses for little to no expense.

To carry this out a survey would need to be completed to identify the following:

Which residents have a college degree;

Which area of study they have a degree in;

If the resident is willing to teach other residents; and

Who is seeking or wanting a college education.

If the survey shows that there are those willing to learn and those who have the education and are willing to teach and the facility has applied for and became a CLEP/DANTES testing center then:

Obtain the CLEP/DANTES study guides;

Have the resident with the degree prepare the lesson plans. Some can be obtained from www.oercommons.org;

Purchases the necessary texts. The resident wanting to take the class can purchase these;

Set the class on the quarterly schedule; and

At the completion of the quarter administer the CLEP/DANTES exam.

In this facility the resident who is willing to teach could be a paid VTP worker, who receives the benefit of a paycheck for his time and effort as an additional incentive and job training tool in preparation for release.

In addition staff can volunteer and take the class as well to earn college credit if the facility allows. This makes this beneficial to the residents, staff of the facility, and society as a whole. In fact classes offered by the program could earn college credits under this system. This would give a resident incentive to attend and add more meaning to the classes.

Graduation Ceremonies

The Program can hold presentation ceremonies where the resident is awarded their degree in a formal fashion as he would if he would have attended the college. This would include the Cap and Gown and the ability to have pictures taken for him to send to family and friends.

What a great step towards self-esteem and meaning in earning an education.

Recognition

Before closing out this proposal I would like to take time to recognize the past efforts of individuals into trying to bring education into this program.

Rob Munden the Department Head for Psychoeducation. He once offered college courses, but due to the cost residents were unable to sign up. It was great of him to try and I hope he can be a part of this in effect to bring what he tried before.

Social Workers of SPTP. They previously put out a survey to try and get a census of who needed a High School Diploma or G.E.D. in the attempts to bring it in this program. I am unsure of what occurred with that but I appreciate your effort.

Tonya Taylor, Program Director SPTP (Past). She graciously approved my requests to seek education and tried to bring the G.E.D. or High School Diploma program in but was shut down. She gave me the ability to learn what I have and present this valid program to the facility. Thank you.

Course Layout

The remainder of this document is the proposed Course Layout for the first course of this proposal.

Lesson 1: Introduction

Welcome to a course to assist you in understanding and knowing how to seek a college education while in SPTP. We hope you find this course informative and helpful in you educational endeavors whatever they may be.

For most they know that college is more schooling after High School. However, this is far from the truth. College is an adventure where one can learn many exciting and new features of the world and how to operate therein. That is why a college offers so many courses to choose from and looks daunting for a person first looking into college.

Now that we have provided you a basis for this class we need to learn what you know or don't know about college. To do this we ask that you fill out this short questionnaire.

Questionnaire
  Please explain in your own words what college is?
  Please explain in your own word what you know about the following terms:
  Credit Hour
  Associate's Degree
  Bachelor's Degree
  Master's Degree
  Doctorate
  Accreditation
  Student Aid
  Scholarship
  Life Experience
  What is the average one would expect to pay for college?
  Does education play a factor in what one can expect to get paid? Please explain.

If there is time remaining go over the answers provided to the questions. The instructor will collect the answers to hold until the end of the quarter for comparison.

Lesson 2: What is College

Most would think of college as a place to learn job skills. While this is true, it is not the whole truth. College can be a way to learn life skills, such as how to do takes, how to invest, banking, cooking, and many more basic life skills.

There are different types of colleges today. Technical or trade schools focus on teaching a particular job trade. This can be welding, construction, roofing, cooking etc. these schools either specialize in one trade or many different trades and offer courses accordingly. They issue certificates more than degrees.

The Junior College is a college that offers classes and degrees. The tuition costs less than what a university costs and usually they offer up to an associate's degree. A University of four year college costs more and offers Bachelor's level degrees.

Then you have graduate school. This can be part of a University or four year college. The cost is higher and they offer Degrees at the Master's and Doctoral level.

Going to college is not automatic. It all begins with an application college. Just like a job you must apply to the school and be accepted. For most schools there is an application fee. In most cases you will be accepted, but keep in mind they can deny your admission.

Now we have learned the differences in colleges but how do we differentiate between what a certificate is and what a degree is? This is a good question and we will go into detail.

A certificate signifies that a person has completed college level work in a specified area. Normally a certificate program requires less than twenty credit hours and each course is specific to the area in which it is entered. Certificates can be earned in many fields, some of the more popular are: Welding, Paralegal, Management, Business, and Computers. A certificate is not as good as a degree but will help one if they are looking for a supervisory position or to work in a certain field. For example, normally a company will not hire a welder unless they have at least a certification in welding.

When you research degrees it is more complicated. There are two divisions the undergraduate and the graduate. Undergraduate consists of Associate's and Bachelor Degrees. Graduate consists of Master's and Doctorate's

An Associate's Degree denotes that the person has completed sixty credit hours of courses. These courses will be specifically listed and defined by the school based on the Degree. An Associate's Degree is divided into an Associate of Art or Associate of Science Degree.

A Bachelor's Degree denotes that the person has completed one-hundred and twenty credit hours of study. To note some schools require the person have an Associate's degree before enrolling in a Bachelor Degree program, always check the requirements of the school. These courses will be specifically listed and defined by the school based on the Degree.

A Master's Degree denotes that the person has completed forty-eight credit hours of specialized study and completed a thesis. In order to enroll in this Degree program you will have to have a Bachelor's Degree and enroll in a graduate school.

A Doctorate denotes that the person has completed thirty-six credit hours of specialized study and completed a dissertation. In order to enroll in this Degree program you will have to have a Master's Degree and enroll in a graduate school.

In discussing the different Degrees we used the term "credit hour." Do you know what this is? Most college courses earn three credit hours upon successful completion. Three credit hours is equivalent to forty-five contact hours. A contact hour is a measure that denotes an hour of scheduled instruction with a student. Therefore, in college a student receives a credit hour if they have a fifty minute classroom session once per week for fifteen weeks, which is a semester.

A semester is what a college splits its course load into. There are generally four semesters a year and some colleges only allow you to enroll in classes at a set time based on their semester start and end times. In addition you normally need to complete your coursework in this time frame as well. Based on this colleges also will limit the total number of classes you can take per semester by limiting the maximum number of credit hours you can take at one time.

In summation there are varying types of degrees that can be earned from college and based on the type of college you may or may not be able to get the degree you want. As such the first step to seeking an education is to define the Degree you want and what type of school you need to seek. This is the first step in an education plan that will be discussed in Lesson 10 and 11.

Lesson 3: Accreditation

As some would say college words are big, daunting, and confusing. This is true until you can learn a proper and adequate definition for the term. In fact it has been shown that when one studies they fail to learn the material because they do not know what a word means. The best study habit is when you see a word you do not know, stop, learn the meaning, and then move on.

The first big word you need to learn about is "Accreditation." Accreditation is the seal of approval a college receives from a board, committee, or group that checks them to see that their methods of educating are proper and actually help the person learn the material. In its simplest form, except in limited circumstances, a degree from a non-accredited educational institute is worthless. This is the second task to finding an appropriate school.

There are two types of accreditation: Governmental and Non-Governmental Accreditation. Governmental Accreditation is what it appears, the government overlooks and monitors the education provided. The benefit to this is that the student would be eligible for student aid offered by the government. This will be discussed more in depth in Lesson 4.

Non-governmental accreditation is an entity other than the government that monitors the school and their method of instruction to ensure that the person will receive a meaningful education.

Based on the accreditation status of the school will also set whether or not the person can earn their degree entirely by correspondence or whether they would have to attend so many hours of class time on campus. Normally only Governmentally Accredited schools would have to require on campus instruction.

If you want to ensure that a Non-Governmental accrediting agency is recognized you can contact either the U.S. Department of Education or the Council for Higher Education Accreditation. These organizations are responsible for oversight of the accrediting agencies and can provide you information as to the legitimacy of the accrediting agency. Their contact info is:

U.S. Department of Education
Accrediting Agency Evaluation Branch
Office of Postsecondary Education
1990 K St. NW
Washington D.C. 20006
(202) 502-7765
www.ed.gov

Council for Higher Education Accreditation
One Dupont Cir. NW Suite 510
Washington D.C. 20036-1136
(202) 955-6126
www.chea.org

In summation accreditation is a seal of approval for the school. It is best that you ensure the school is accredited before beginning course work so you can ensure it is not a waste of your time or money.

Lesson 4: Financing an Education

One of the reasons most do not seek an education is because the cost of a college education is high. A junior college is the cheapest and it goes up from there. Colleges charge per credit hour and this does not include the required textbooks, which range from $50.00 up to $300.00 or more per book.

Your first thought is, "Well I am done, I cannot afford this." You may be right, except that is an improper though for herein we will discuss and show you ways to cut the cost of your education.

The costs involved include application fees, shipping expenses, textbooks and tuition. Keep in mind an inmate in a correctional facility, who makes $20.00 a month, can afford an education. If they can you can.

To help you understand how to manage the expense we will go over the following: (1) Waiver; (2) Scholarship/Grant; (3) Federal Student Aid; (4) Exams in Lieu of Coursework; (5) Credit Bank Schools; (6) Textbook Cost Reduction; (7) Life Experience; and (8) Taxes.

Waiver

Most schools have an application or course registration fee. Though the school, does not inform possible students, they will waive these fees for those who are on a financial hardship. One just has to ask for a waiver of the fee. It is better to ask than not to ask for it can save you on your expense.

Scholarship/Grant

A scholarship or grant is where a person, entity, or group volunteers to pay the costs for your education. Most of these require an application process and then are awarded only to a select few individuals. If given these are not required to be paid back.

As a confined person there are practically none of these types of aid available and if they are the cost, time, and effort will more often than not make them unfeasible.

Federal Student Aid

In 1993 the United States Congress passed legislation barring all confined persons from receiving Federal Student Aid. This law was reversed in the year 2020 by the United States Congress. It is estimated that it will take until the year 2023 for the Department of Education to restore this to those confined.

Once restored in order to see what Federal Student Aid you are eligible for, you will need to: (1) Check with the educational institution; and (2) Fill out and submit a Free Application for Student Aid (FAFSA).

Most educational institutions do not participate in Federal Student Aid. Currently Adams State University in Colorado does participate and offers classes to those confined.

Keep in mind that some Federal Student Aid is required to be paid back. Pay close attention to the information that is provided when you apply or accept any Federal Student Aid.

Exams in Lieu of Courses

One can cut costs by taking an exam instead of a course and receive full credit as if the course was taken. These are referred to as: (1) CLEP/ DANTES; (2) Equivalence exams; and (3) Challenge exams.

In order to see if these or others are accepted look at the information received from the education institution you are looking at attending. Sometimes you may have to specifically ask if they offer this type of service.

As with anything there is a limit as to how many credits you can replace with exams. However, even though it is limited it still reduces the cost for your education.

Credit Bank Schools

A school that has no limit on credit transfers, exams for credits, or portfolio credits is known as a credit bank school. They allow for a person to transfer all they have from any source and apply it towards a degree.

They usually require one to take at least one or more courses to be awarded a degree. This means the cost is very low. However, keep in mind these types of schools have a bad reputation and some employers will not recognize the degrees issued by them.

Textbooks

Textbooks are a very expensive part of a college education. There are ways to save costs in this area, such as: (1) Rental; (2) ILL; (3) Book share; (4) Used; and (5) Buyback.

Textbook rental is offered by a few schools or textbook stores. Under this one is usually required to put a safety deposit in and then pay a fee for each book rented. This can reduce the cost of a book from $200.00 to $35.00.

Inter Library Loan (ILL) can be used to get textbooks. The issue here is that you only have the book for about two weeks and renewal is not an option. It is free and for the confined person with a lot of time on their hands this may be a good option.

Book share is where: (1) Two or more people share the cost of one book and each use it; or (2) When one donates a textbook for others to use. This reduces the costs of the textbook, but one needs to ensure they follow the rules of the facility in doing this.

Used textbooks can be purchased for a fraction of the cost. The downfall is that they usually are marked with pen, pencil, or highlighter. Even though it is marked, which can help you study, this is a great reduction in the cost of a textbook.

Some college bookstores will buy the textbooks back from you. This allows for you to recoup your costs. Always check to see if this is true and what they will pay you for the text. In addition www.textbooks.com does buy college textbooks back.

Life Experience

Life experience is credit for something you have done during your life. In order to receive this you must show how it gave you experience or skills comparable to that which a college student would have learned by taking a course.

This requires you to meticulously and fully explain the life experience and what you learned or did in writing. It is an application process for which some schools charge a fee for evaluating your submission.

Taxes

At the end of the year everyone hates tax time. However, for a student there is certain credits and refunds they receive for attending school. This means some of what you spent during the year can be recovered. For more information refer to the current tax rules.

Lesson 5:   High School

In order to enroll in college most schools require that the person have a High School Diploma or G.E.D. in requiring this, the school will require you to submit a copy of it when you apply for admission to the school.

For some in this program they already have a High School Diploma or G.E.D. and for others they do not. This lesson will be tailored to both types.

For those who have received a High School Diploma or G.E.D. and do not have a copy, they can receive one by writing the school that issued it. If they do not know the address or the school is no longer in existence they can write to the Board of Education for the State in which they received the High School Diploma or G.E.D. If you need assistance with this please put in a request to speak with the social worker. There should be no cost for the receipt of this document and at times one can even receive their transcript.

For those who do not have a High School Diploma or G.E.D. they will first need to acquire one before moving on to college. This will require that they seek out a correspondence school that offers this service. Some of the schools still offering this are as follows:

American School, Independent Study Division, 2200 East 170th Street, Lansing Illinois 60438; (708) 418-2850; www.americanschool.org

Brigham Young University, Independent Study, ATTN: High-School Programs, 120 Morris Center, Provo Utah 84602; (801) 422-2868; www.elearn.byu.edu

Citizens High School, 188 College Drive, PO Box 66089, Orange Park, Florida 32065-6089; (904) 276-1700; www.citizenshighschool.com

Griggs International Academy, 8903 U.S. Highway 31, Berrien Spring Michigan 49104; (269) 471-6570; www.griggs.edu

North Dakota Center for Distance Education, 4776 28th Avenue South, Fargo North Dakota 58104; (704) 298 4830; www.ndcde.org

Stratford Career Institute, 1 Champlain Commons Unit 3, Saint Albans Vermont 05478-5560; www.scitraining.com

Keep in mind this information may be old and the schools may have decided to no longer offer it. A resident will need to contact them and receive information as to their cost and what they offer.

Lesson 6:   Schools and Options

The discussion thus far has been all about what you can and cannot do and defining necessary terms. It is now time to discuss the options available to you and schools that are available. This will help you define and begin to start to set a plan in place.

Schools that are not accredited

As discussed earlier a school that lacks accreditation usually allows you to earn degrees and credits that are not transferrable. Dependent on the school the employer may not accept it as well. You may ask then why are we spending time discussing it?

A school that lacks accreditation cannot charge as much for their education as a school that is accredited, therefore it is a cheaper option. In addition you can take courses that may prepare you to take an exam in lieu of a course. This then means the course is cheaper.

An example of this is one takes and receives a certificate in accounting from an unaccredited school. Later they enroll in an accredited school that accepts exams in lieu of courses. The person requests the exam for accounting and passes. He is awarded 3 Credit hours for the course. At the unaccredited school the cost was $400.00, but to take the course at the accredited school would have cost him $600.00 or more, and then textbooks. So he saves no less than $200.00.

Do not shy away from an a school that is not accredited, just do your research and ensure the investment is a savings somewhere down the road. Also, keep in mind an unaccredited school may be the only one that offers what you seek. At this point the option is yours.

Adams State University

This University is located in Colorado and has been serving the confined person for over twenty years. They charge $220.00 per credit hour and their school bookstore does buy books back. They participate in Federal Financial Aid and veteran's benefits.

The degrees they offer is mostly focused on Business, but they offer the same courses as a normal university. All exams are proctored and they do accept CLEP/DANTES and life experience credits. The highest degree awarded is a Master's.

In addition one can earn a paralegal degree and advanced paralegal degree. The paralegal degree puts six credits towards any degree and the advanced paralegal degree adds an additional eighteen credit hours towards any degree.

They enroll on a semester schedule and one must enroll at the start of a semester. You can take individual courses or enroll as a student and seek a degree. At $220.00 per credit hour an associate's degree is $13,200.00 plus the cost of books. They do not have a payment plan option.

California Coast University

This school has been allowing those confined, the military and many others to earn college degrees or diplomas since the '80's. They charge $150.00 per credit hour and have a payment plan, but no federal student aid option. One can earn a Doctorate through this school.

This school accepts CLEP/DANTES, transfer credit, and challenge exams. All exams are proctored, but they are more lenient as to who the proctor can be. They have tuition discounts for certain persons and do accept veteran's benefits for payment.

They have an option to earn an Undergraduate or Graduate level Diploma in different fields. The cost for this is around $2,000.00 and is equal to about twelve credit hours. These can be applied later to a degree if one wishes to pursue that at a later time.

Blackstone Career Institute

Offers a degree in Paralegal for about $850.00. they do not participate in Federal Financial aid but do accept veteran's benefits. Once graduated the individual can earn an advanced paralegal degree. They offer two different payment plans and prepare one to sit for a Paralegal certification through a national licensing organization.

Lesson 7: What an Education Plan is

In this we will begin the discussion on what an education plan is. As with most things in life planning is key to ensuring that we can accomplish something. When it comes to seeking an education there is no differe3nce, planning is key.

The Education Plan is a roadmap that you will use to outline exactly what you want to accomplish and how you will achieve each part of the Education Plan to achieve the ultimate goal, an education. It is easy to just jump into this without a plan and without any research, but they

SEXUALLY VIOLENT OFFENDER

usually is fraught with roadblocks and issues.

When you add confinement to the mix it becomes even more complicated without an Education Plan because you may enter into something that is not allowed or in the end will not work out with the facility. One must be careful to plan.

An example education plan is as follows:

Joe Bob
1301 K264 HWY 264
Larned Kansas 67550

EDUCATION PLAN

Education Sought: AutoCAD Drafter
Research Results:
Plum University, 123 Oakmont, Kansas 67450. Total cost $4,050.00. Requires computer and software. Tests are proctored. Must have access to internet to submit work. Accredited. Payments of $150.00 per month.

Prune University, 126 Slowmont Avenue, Kansas 67250. Total cost $2,225.00 plus books. No computer needed but drawing equipment is needed. Fill in test sheets submitted to school via mail. Not accredited. Payment plan: $25.00 down and $60.00 per month.

State University, 129 Speedy Avenue, Kansas 67150. Total cost $9,000.00. requires computer, software and internet. Accredited. Payment plan not available.

Budget:
I currently work 14 hours per week at $7.35 per hour. This is $102.90 a week, $411.60 a month. My monthly expenses are $292.30 so I have $119.30 to spend each month. In addition I received $400.00 in taxes this year.

Facility Rules:
Property Variance needed to work with the school.
Property variance needed for textbooks.
Media Request needed for each textbook.
Internet not allowed.
No computer and no software
Drawing utensils limited based on what they are.

Goals:
Set aside one hour per day for study
Set aside two hours when it is time to test.
Complete one to three lessons every two weeks.
Attempt the work on my own before asking for help

Feasibility:
In accords with the research and the information I have I could afford Prune University but it may be denied dependent upon the drawing materials. Per the rules of the facility I cannot take the course from Plum or State University. It appears as if this is not a feasible education path. I may wish to seek other options.

Action Plan:
As this was not feasible I will start a new plan and try to find a different education track that will work.

In the next lesson we will discuss each section in detail and start working towards an education plan for each person.
Lesson 8:   Parts of an Education Plan
In the last lesson we discussed an Education Plan and gave an example of one. Now we are going to discuss the different parts of an education plan.

From the example provided you notice that the first part is to put your name and address on the right side of the upper part of page one. This allows for a reader to identify who is preparing the plan and who it is for.

The first section to fill in is titled: "Education Sought." This short be a short title listing exactly what you seek as an education or degree. It ultimately sets the purpose for the plan and defines what the other sections will discuss.

The second section is: "Research Results." Once you defined the purpose, what you seek, you have to research your options to fulfill that purpose. The results of your research after contacting schools and reading their literature is listed here. You should list all of them, no matter if they are positive or not. This way you can see all options at a quick glance.

The third section is: "Budget." In this you do not have to do a massive detail of all your expenses and assets. It just needs a quick cap of what you can currently afford to pay for education. When you have defined the amount you can put forward each month this will help you limit your "research results" even further. Keep in mind any change in your financial status that may be seen in the future.

The fourth section is: "Facility Rules." As a confined person this is important for you must remain within the rules of the facility in seeking your education. This section allows you to make notes from your review of the pertinent rules. One who reviews the plan may be able to identify some rule that you may have missed or forgot. This will assist in receiving approval prior to starting.

The fifth section is: "Goals." The goal is an education but what goals are needed to ensure that you can meet the main goal. Some areas to discuss are study habits, financial obligations, compliance with rules, and the amount of time you would like to be completing the courses and lessons. There can be many goals and each should be specific and identifiable to the point that one can track and see if you are meeting them.

The sixth section is: "Feasibility." In this section you will review all previous sections and state whether or not what you seek can be accomplished. There are times, as shown in the example, when the answer will be that it cannot be done. Do not let this frustrate you, just start a new plan until this section shows that it can be done. Trial and error are the best teachers and will help you formulate the best plan before seeking your education.

The last section is: "Action Plan." In this you will list step by step how you will set the plan into fruition or if the plan is not feasible a notice that you recognize this and how you plan to move forward with a new plan. This will be detailed and lengthy based upon what you are seeking.

Now that we have discussed the parts and shown an example to you, your homework for the week is to create an education plan and bring it to the next class session. We are aware you may not be able to complete all sections, but please complete all sections to the best of your ability.

Lesson 9: Education Plan Creation

Go over and review each person's education plan they brought. Try to broaden their horizons if they are unsure as to what is available to them.

Lesson 10: Education Resume/Portfolio

Another important document they you will need to create is known as an Education Resume or Portfolio. Like a job resume this is a document that highlights all your education and experience, but in a different format. This document is presented when you apply for admission to a school.

This is meant to be very detailed and meticulous. It should always be in chronological order and highlight all the important facts. Here are some good and bad examples of entries in a Education Resume or Portfolio.

Bad Example

Dietary Department, 2010-2018. Cooked and served meals.

Vocational Degree, 2003. Computers.

Certificate of Completion, Ethics, 2020.

Good Example

Job: Dietary Department Time: 2010-2018

Education: Learned how to read a recipe, do basic math in converting decimals and fractions to increase or decrease the amount in a recipe. Did some inventory management to ensure the product was present for the meal. Worked with medical orders from a doctor to ensure individuals were properly fed. Completed my work in a clean and sanitary environment, after being taught proper cleaning procedures. Interpersonal skills were used daily as I worked with different people and customers.

Vocational Degree: Computers Completed: 2003 With Honors

Areas Covered: Desktop publishing using Microsoft Office (Word and Excel). Internet usage and searching through search engines like Bing and Google. Installation and removal of basic components (i.e. HDD Drives, CD-Rom, etc.) . Learn and practiced using scanners and printers of all types.

Certificate: Ethics Year: 2020

Information: A therapy course led by an instructor with a college degree. They taught the basics of Ethics and what they are and how they apply. It was a twelve week course that met for one hour per week.

The bad examples are not wrong, they just will earn you nothing. They show laziness and a lack of wanting to put a good foot forward. They also will not cause a school to want to offer any credit for life experience or an exam in lieu of a course.

The good examples are not only true but are a very good indication of why credit should be given. It allows the reviewer to apply the facts to a course and find that you may not need a course. The more time and effort you put in the better it is for you and the more you can save towards the cost of your education.

Now that we have discussed and shown how not to prepare an Education resume/Portfolio and how to prepare a good one, your homework is to create one and bring it to the next class session. At that time we will go over and review them.

Lesson 11:   Education Resume/Portfolio Review

Go over and review each person's Education Resume/Portfolio they brought. Try to broaden their horizons if they are unsure as to what is available to them.

Lesson 12:   Review

Welcome to the last day of this class. In this we have provided you the information available to succeed and seek a high school diploma or college degree while in this program. You have an Education Plan and Education Resume/Portfolio. The ball is now in your court to put this into action. The second part of this class is where this occurs and you are now eligible for this.

If need be do a final review of Education Plan and Education Resume/Portfolio for each person or if they have questions answer them if able.

We will now have you answer the questionnaire that you did at the beginning of the quarter to see what you have learned.

Questionnaire

    Please explain in your own words what college is?

    Please explain in your own word what you know about the following terms:

    Credit Hour

    Associate's Degree

    Bachelor's Degree

    Master's Degree

    Doctorate

    Accreditation

    Student Aid

    Scholarship

    Life Experience

    What is the average one would expect to pay for college?

Does education play a factor in what one can expect to get paid? Please explain.

We wish you luck in your educational endeavors and know that we will help to the best of our ability. Thank you for taking this class.

SEXUALLY VIOLENT OFFENDER

www.ingramcontent.com/pod-product-compliance
Lightning Source LLC
Chambersburg PA
CBHW060317030426
42336CB00011B/1084